UNIVERSITY OF NORTH CAROLINA
STUDIES IN THE ROMANCE LANGUAGES AND LITERATURES
Number 49

A HISTORY OF THE *USELESS PRECAUTION*
PLOT IN SPANISH AND FRENCH LITERATURE

A HISTORY OF THE *USELESS PRECAUTION* PLOT IN SPANISH AND FRENCH LITERATURE

BY

FRANK SEDWICK

CHAPEL HILL
THE UNIVERSITY OF NORTH CAROLINA PRESS

DEPÓSITO LEGAL: v. 2.067 - 1964
ARTES GRÁFICAS SOLER, S. A. — VALENCIA — 1964

CONTENTS

	Page
INTRODUCTION ...	9
FIRST SPANISH ARTISTIC DEVELOPMENTS OF THE THEME: DECEIVED HUSBANDS AND DECEIVED BROTHERS ...	17
I. Cervantes' *Cueva de Salamanca* ...	17
II. Cervantes' *El viejo celoso* ...	18
III. Cervantes' *El celoso extremeño* ...	19
IV. More Deceived Husbands ...	24
V. The Deceived-Brother Plays ...	27
DORIMOND. MOLIÈRE: DECEIVED GUARDIANS ...	38
I. *L'école des maris* ...	39
II. *L'école des femmes* ...	45
III. *Le sicilien* ...	47
IN THE WAKE OF MOLIÈRE ...	49
SUMMARY ...	80
BIBLIOGRAPHY ...	82
Books ...	82
Articles ...	84

REPRESENTATIVE SPANISH AND FRENCH USELESS-PRECAUTION WORKS

	WORK AND DATE	TYPE	GO-BETWEEN	BRIBE OR REWARD?	DISGUISE OF GALLANT OR GO-BETWEEN	MARRY TOMORROW?	CUCKOLD TAKE TRIP?	LETTER(S) GALLANT TO GIRL & VICE VERSA?	NOTARY?	DETAILS OF PRECAUTIONS?	ARRIVAL OF POLICE AT END?	DISGUISE OF CUCKOLD?
Earliest period of the theme in the Spanish language.	*Ensemplo* XC	husband-wife	none	none	none	no	yes	no	no	no	no	none
	Ensemplo XCI	husband-wife	mother-in-law	none	none ("hermano")	no	yes	no	no	no	no	none
	Ensemplo CCCXXXV	husband-wife	none	none	none	no	no	no	no	yes	no	none
Impetus of Cervantes: deceived husbands.	Cervantes: *La cueva de Salamanca* c.1611	husband-wife	Cristina	none	none	no	yes	no	no	no	no	none
	Cervantes: *El viejo celoso* c.1612	husband-wife	Hortigosa	none	none (tapestry)	no	yes	no	no	yes	yes	none
	Cervantes: *El celoso extremeño* 1613	husband-wife	1. Luis 2. Marialonso	yes; bribe	go-between; beggar-musician	no	no (before marriage)	no	no	yes	no	none
	Zayas: *El prevenido, engañado* 1657 or earlier	husband-wife	*"ama vecina"*	none	none	no	yes	no	no	no	no	none
	Scarron: *La précaution inutile* 1655	husband-wife	a neighbor	none	none	no	yes	no	no	no	no	none
The Lope derivatives: deceived brother.	Lope: *El mayor imposible* 1615	brother-sister	Ramón (gracioso)	yes	Lisardo (gallant): "guapeja" Ramón (gracioso): messenger or squire	no	no	yes	no	no	no	none
	Boes-Robert: *La folle gageure* 1653	brother-sister	Philipin (valet)	yes	gallant: none Philipin: 1. merchant, 2. squire	no	no	yes	no	no	no	none
	Moreto: *No puede ser* 1661	brother-sister	Tarugo (gracioso)	yes	gallant: none, enters house unobserved Tarugo: *sastre*, *italiano*	yes, but not the sister	no	yes	no	no	no	none
	Favorolhi: *La précaution inutile* 1692	brother-sister	many	yes	many	yes	no	yes	no	no	no	coachman
	Dortmond: *La femme industrieuse* 1661	husband-wife (freed slave)	doctor (inadvertently)	none	gallant: phantom (for his exit)	no, but *demain* not mentioned	no	no	no	no (except armed guards)	no	none
The period of Dortmond and Molière.	Dortmond: *L'école des cocus* 1661	husband-wife	none	none	none	yes, *demain* not	yes	no	no	no	no	none
	Molière: *L'école des maris* 1661	guardian-ward	none	none	none	yes	no	yes	yes	no	no	music
	Molière: *L'école des femmes* 1662	guardian-ward	servants	yes	gallant: artist	yes	no	yes	yes	yes	no	music
	Molière: *Le Sicilien* 1667	(freed slave)	Hali	none	Hali: music virtuoso, Spanish gentlemen	no	no	no	no	no	no	none
	Nanteuil: *L'amour sentinelle* 1669	guardian-ward	Crocin (valet) helps	yes	gallant, valet: house guards	no	no	yes	no	no	no	wearer
	Champmeslé: *La Fleurutla* 1683	guardian-ward	none	yes	none	"ce soir"	no	yes	no	no	yes	doctor
	Dancourt: *Le tuteur* 1695	guardian-ward	L'Olive (valet)	none	gallant: painter; valet: gardener	yes first "soon," then "today," then "ce soir"	no	no	yes	no	no	female
	Dancourt: *Colin-maillard* 1701	guardian-ward	Mme. Brillard (the aunt); Lépine (valet) helps	none	gallant: peasant	yes	yes	no	yes	no	no	none
Representative works post-Molière: guardian and ward.	Regnard: *Les folies amoureuses* 1704	guardian-ward	Nonce, but Lisette and Crispin help	yes	none	no	no	yes	no	yes	no	male
	Valé: *Le peintre* 1752	guardian-ward	none	none	gallant: as a servant and simpleton	yes	no	no	no	no	no	none
	Rochon de la Valette: *L'école des mœurs* 1754	guardian-ward	Bellumier	yes	Bellumier: public official	no	no	yes, message on cap	no	no	no	female
	Guadlerre: *Rosaide à la mode* 1762	guardian-ward	Arlequin (valet)	none	gallant: merchant; apothecary Arlequin: animal, merchant	"ce soir"	no	yes	no	no	no	female
	Clément: *La pipée* 1756	guardian-ward	none	none	none	yes	no	no	no	no	no	music
	Anseaulh: *Les précautions inutiles* 1760	guardian-ward	none	none	none	no	no	no	no	no	no	none
	Sedaine: *On ne s'avise jamais de tout* 1761	guardian-ward	none, unless danger unexpectedly	none	gallant: *domestique*, *cupid*, *tatelle*	"ce soir"	no	no	no	yes	yes	none
	Cailhava: *Le tuteur dupé* 1765	guardian-ward	Merlin (valet)	yes	gallant: painter	"ce soir"	yes	no	no	no	no	none
	Beaumarchais: *Le barbier de Séville* 1775	guardian-ward	Figaro	yes, to both Figaro & Bazile	gallant: soldier; music master	yes	no	yes	yes	yes	yes	none
	Gonsález del Castillo: *La inocente Dorotea* c.1800	guardian-ward	Pedro (valet); & (*lucía*)	yes	Pedro: as servant to the guardian	"cazarnos hoy sin falta"	no	no	yes	no	no	angel
	Delavigne: *L'école des vieillards* 1823	husband-wife	none	none	none	no	no	yes (but not delivered)	no	no	no	none

A full-size version of this chart is available to view at:
https://www.uncpress.org/sedwick_insert_p7-8/

INTRODUCTION

Reference is intended to a theme like that of what might be termed its end product, the *Barber of Seville*: sequestered young wife or ward and her lover who, usually aided by a go-between, match wits with the elderly and jealous husband or guardian of the girl, and a plot whose focal point of action is the gallant's contrivance to enter the protector's house. It would be pointless to attempt an interrelation of all types of cuckolds, jealous protectors, and vigilant fathers in the long history of a nation's literature. The present intention is to deal with a specific aspect of cuckoldry, the one in which cuckolding is the final result of a dramatic plot that rotates about a common axis—the aforementioned gallant's conspiracy to enter the house, for this is a theme whose variants have a traceable literary history.

The word *cuckold* is used here only through linguistic lack of a more all-inclusive term. By definition a cuckold must be married, yet Beaumarchais' Don Bartholo, for example, is not yet married to Rosine. It will be evident, however, that the general nature of the theme is little affected by the specific type of relationship as long as a jealous and frequently greedy husband, brother, or guardian exhibits undue restraint upon his female charge and finally becomes the victim of his own useless precautions in guarding the girl.

Questions of influence from author to author inevitably arise as we trace the history of an idea. Genesis and parallelism are the essence of this type of study—the origin, dissemination, and ultimate exhaustion of a type of plot—especially in so far as they reveal the degree of skill with which new and pirated elements are blended in a given version of the theme. None of this investigation is done, however, in a spirit of literary sleuthing whereby the cop-critic catches the robber-writer. Theft is unimportant here, except as study of the literary spoilage will reveal motive and consequence germane to the total history of the theme. Before proceeding with the life history, it will be well to catalog the anatomy of this plot which in the twentieth century is now a corpse.

The first of the standardized characters is the repressed wife, ward, or sister who is frequently very young, usually simple or innocent at first, sometimes becoming openly defiant and aggressive, but always clever ultimately in getting her man, for *El mayor imposible*, as Lope de Vega entitled his version of the theme, is the task of guarding a woman when she does not wish to be guarded; or as Inés says in Act I of Calderón's *El alcalde de Zalamea: Mas tengo por disparate/ El guardar a una mujer/ Si ella no quiere guardarse.* One of the variants in the many manifestations of the theme is the type of foil for the maiden. He is an elderly guardian in Molière and most later works; he is an elderly husband in the early works like those of Cervantes; in Lope and works derived from Lope he is the girl's brother. Whatever his function, he is always cuckolded.

The elderly protector is invariably of the Bartholo type: jealous, boorish, selfish, even corrupt, but blundering, and himself desirous of marrying his ward, often to lay hands on her money. Jealousy is his most unbridled fault as emphasized in the extreme measures he takes to guard the house. From the point of view of dramatic construction, the guardian must have sufficient faults to justify the ward's rebelliousness; in fact, he must be stupid when he is to be the dupe of what is often a thirteen- or fourteen-year-old girl, lest her ability to deceive border on the improbable.

The gallant usually wishes to marry the girl. This desire is mutual, and in later versions the marriage is facilitated at the end, sometimes by the arrival of a notary; but in several of the early works, like Cervantes' *El celoso extremeño*, the gallant is merely attempting to make a conquest. A duenna, a neighbor, a valet, or various other servants often aid the gallant in his intrigue to gain admittance to the house. This enterprise is, as already mentioned, the pivot of the drama.

Since the house is always so well sealed and sentinelled by the guardian, the gallant often seeks the aid of a confidant. Spanish Golden Age drama with its customary *gracioso* was well disposed to supply a comic version of that role which on the French stage emerged as the valet, under the influence of the intriguing Arlecchino and the *commedia dell'arte*. Still the go-between is not essential to the theme, for in certain versions the girl and her gallant find their own means. Nonetheless, by the time of Beaumarchais the role of confidant had developed into the major proportions of a Figaro.

These are the essential characters as they have become stereotyped, but in its period of formation the theme had only a husband and a wife. The simple cuckolding of the husband occurs repeatedly in the stories of Antiquity, folklore, and the Middle Ages, so frequently that the prototype cuckold seems to be inextricable from the maze of stories. Interested readers are referred to the Stith Thompson and John Keller Motif-Indexes of, respectively, Folk-Literature and mediaeval Spanish *exempla*. Inasmuch as the present concern is with just one line of development of the theme, in what might be called the later sophisticated literature (and that, only of France and Spain), it may be sufficient to give merely one or two examples from the Middle Ages and point out only one all-important collection of stories: the *Disciplina Clericalis*, the source for many similar examples in the later *Libro de los gatos, Calila y Dimna, Castigos y documentos,* Alfonso's *Cantigas, Libro de los engaños,* and others.

In the Spanish language, probably one of the earliest embryonic forms of the theme is to be found in three of the stories in the *Libro de los enxemplos* (early fifteenth century) by Clemente Sánchez de Vercial.[1] This collection is the most extensive of the Spanish as well as many European collections of *exempla* in the vernacular. *Exemplum* was used in the sense of a tale with a moral. Many of these *exempla*, whose sources will be discussed, are

---

[1] SÁNCHEZ DE VERCIAL was born about 1370 and composed the *Libro de los enxemplos,* of which two manuscripts are extant, between 1400 and 1421. See Alexandre Haggerty Krappe, "Les sources du *Libro de exemplos*," *Bulletin Hispanique*, Vol. XXXIX (1937), 5-34; also John E. Keller, "The *Libro de los exenplos por a. b. c.*," *Hispania*, Vol. XL, No. 2 (May, 1957), 179-186.

common to all of mediaeval Europe; but it will be shown how the theme made its way to France through Spanish developments from the *exempla*,[2] and embellished with elements and character types from the Italian *commedia dell'arte* of later times. One of the three *exempla* chosen from the *Libro de los enxemplos*, number XCI (Gayangos) or CLXII (Keller)[3] is short enough to be reproduced here in its entirety:

> Dizen que un ombre partio de su cassa para yr camino, e comendo su mugier a su suegra; e la mugier amava a otro mas que a su marido. E la madre dixo al amigo commo el marido de su fija era ydo, e un dia convidolo. E ellos estando comiendo, vino el marido e llamo a la puerta. E la mugier llevantosse apriessa e ascondio al amigo e despues fuesse a la puerta abrir al marido. E de que entro mando que le aparejassen el lecho que venia cansado e queria folgar. La mugier non sabia que se fazer, e dixole la madre:
> "Non aparejes el lecho fasta que mostremos a tu marido el lienço que fezimos."

---

[2] This does not mean that the Latin *exempla* common in France were lacking specimens of the unfaithful wife who tricks her husband. For instance, in the *exemplum* CCXXX of the *Sermones Vulgares* of Jaques de Vitry, a wife is overzealously guarded by her husband and is motivated to deceive him as follows: While out with her husband, she allows herself to fall in the mud outside a certain house where she has instructed her lover to wait. She asks her husband to wait outside while she enters the house to remove and clean her dress. She visits with her lover, comes out with a clean dress, and in this way cuckolds her husband. (There are versions of this *exemplum*, as well as other similar unfaithful-wife tales, in *Les cent nouvelles nouvelles*, from which la Fontaine took his *conte: On ne s'avise jamais de tout*, not to be confused with the play of the same name by Sedaine which will be studied here.) Our theme requires, however, more than an unfaithful wife. She should introduce her lover into her own house, often despite the enumerated precautions of her husband. Although her adulterous action will seem almost to be justified as a symbol of protest against the jealous husband's curtailment of a wife's freedom, it will be seen that the intrigue for the gallant to enter and leave the house is the core of the theme under present scrutiny.

[3] It is number XCI in *Biblioteca de autores españoles*, Vol. LI (Madrid, 1860), *Escritores en prosa anteriores al siglo XV*, p. 469, edited by Pascual de Gayangos. I have preferred to reproduce the text of the *exemplum* as it is given in John E. Keller's new and probably definitive edition of the *Libro de los exenplos por a. b. c.* (Madrid, 1961), p. 134, where it is numbered 162.

INTRODUCTION 13

E la vieja saco el lienço, e tomo el un cabo e dio el otro a la fija, e estendieronlo delante del marido e tovieronlo tanto extendido fasta que se fue el que estava ascondido.
E dixo la madre a la fija: "Estiende esta savana que tu e yo filamos e teximos sobre la cama de tu marido."
E el dixo a la suegra: "¿E tu sabes fazer tal lienço?"
E dixo ella: "O fijo, muchas tales commo este he yo fecho e aparejado."

Bonilla y San Martín points out [4] that this *exemplum* is the basis for an *entremés* by Cervantes entitled *El viejo celoso*, which will be examined presently. The *exemplum* itself is taken from the tale numbered X (numbers IX and XI are also deceived-husband tales) in the previous *Disciplina Clericalis* by the Aragonese Jew Petrus Alphonsi (Pedro Alfonso), born 1062, converted 1106. The *Disciplina* is of course written in Latin, but it is generally believed to have been composed originally in Hebrew or Arabic and then translated to Latin for purposes of popularization. Pascual de Gayangos, editor of the *Biblioteca de autores españoles* edition of the *Disciplina*, holds this view and further states that a certain flavor produced by turns of phrase and choice of words would indicate that the original text was in Arabic rather than Hebrew. [5] Even researchers who are not mediaevalists know the *Disciplina Clericalis* to be "the oldest of Occidental story-books". [6] Whatever their earliest linguistic vehicle, the materials of the *Disciplina* are essentially Eastern and surely taken from Arabic books common at the time, one of them the collection of stories known as *Makáyidu-n-nisá* or the *Deceits of Women*. Menéndez Pelayo is not alone in asserting (see fn. 5) that most Arabic stories came from Persia

---

[4] ADOLFO BONILLA Y SAN MARTÍN, *Entremeses de Miguel de Cervantes Saavedra* (Madrid, 1916), pp. 242-243. See also Georges Cirot, "Gloses sur les 'maris jaloux' de Cervantes," *Bulletin Hispanique*, Vol. XXXI (1929), p. 4.
[5] *Biblioteca de autores españoles*, Vol. LI, p. 444. See also the "Juicio de Menéndez Pelayo sobre la *Disciplina Clericalis*," pp. xxxv-xxxviii of the bilingual (Latin and Spanish) edition of the *Disciplina* by Angel González Palencia (Madrid: Granada, 1948). González Palencia reproduced the Hilka and Söderhjelm text *Die Disciplina Clericalis des Petrus Alfonsi* of Heidelberg, 1911.
[6] FLORENCE N. JONES, *Beaumarchais and Plautus: The Sources of the Barbier de Séville* (Chicago, 1908), p. 25.

and India. It is thus quite likely that the *exemplum* XCI and others like it have their ultimate origin in the Orient.

It is as possibly the main link between the literature of the Orient and that of the Western peoples that the *Disciplina* is of greatest importance. It should be pointed out, however, that since the 1489 print of the *Ysopete Ystoriado* contains the first printed versions of the *Disciplina*, the *Ysopete* was probably a main source for such stories as utilized by Spanish *Siglo de Oro* authors, who probably did not read many manuscripts. The *Disciplina* is known to be the common source of much of the material of the *Gesta Romanorum*, the *Canterbury Tales*, the *Decameron*, and other such collections. In the pages to follow, frequent reference will be made to Boccaccio's *Decameron*, written 1348-1353, which exhibits a plethora of cuckolds, especially among the stories of the Seventh Day. It should be borne in mind, however, that the *Decameron* postdates the *Gesta Romanorum* and other works (but not Chaucer's), and that among Boccaccio's varied sources were these same mediaeval tales in Latin or Italian with their Roman or Oriental origin.

Another significant early ancestor of our theme is the narrative embodied in Plautus' *Amphitryon*, c. 186 B.C. In order to possess Alcmena, wife of Amphitryon, none other than Jupiter himself assumes the husband's form while the husband is away at war. To aid Jupiter, Mercury assumes the role of Amphitryon's servant named Soria. Much confusion occurs when Amphitryon comes home and Jupiter hides in the attic. In the end, Jupiter identifies himself and all turns out well, because Amphitryon has been cuckolded by none less than the king of the gods.

This play has been reworked extensively in modern times in all the principal languages of Europe (e. g., versions by Juan de Timoneda, Francisco López de Villalobos, Hernán Pérez de Oliva, Camões, Routrou, Giraudoux, Molière, Dryden, von Kleist), but in perpetuating the fantastic element it has usually taken an independent course from the branch of the cuckold theme under present scrutiny. Although Plautus' *Amphitryon* is presumed to have had a lost Greek original, the myth is even older than that, being among the most ancient fables of India. Once again the path leads to the East.

The *Miles gloriosus* by the same Plautus is also a much imitated work and, through the Italian *commedia dell'arte*, is a remote ancestor of the later European works, especially the French ones. It is the story of a soldier, Pyrgopolynices, who is duped into losing the young slave girl whom he has kidnapped from a young Athenian who loves her. Presumably this play gave to the *commedia dell'arte* one of its stock characters: the braggart captain, what the French call the *soldat fanfaron*. (We shall see him as the cuckolded husband in two of Dorimond's useless-precaution comedies.) Aside from the general aspect of all kinds of "duping," so common in the Italian scenarios, and so much imitated on the French stage of the seventeenth and eighteenth centuries, the main contribution of the *commedia dell'arte* to the useless-precaution plot is its character types. Besides the swaggering captain, for which, by the way, the Italians had first-hand models among the Spanish troops in Italy during the fifteenth and sixteenth centuries, there is also the *dottore* (often cuckolded in the Italian scenarios), the lascivious and greedy old Pantalone, or the Brighella kind of villain who evolved into Molière's Sganarelle. All of these are evident, at one time or another, or sometimes fused, in the role equivalent to that of Bartholo in Beaumarchais' version of the theme.

Italian troupes went to both Spain and France. In France they arrived about the middle of the sixteenth century and enjoyed an increasing vogue until the government banned them in 1697 because of their mounting tendency to lewd performances. In 1716, however, they returned to the Théâtre Italien where they became well established again. During the time that the Italian companies were in Paris, their improvised comedies were produced alongside of and in competition with the wholly-written conventional type of stage production. Even Molière, whose guardian-and-ward plays will be examined, began his career under the influence of the *commedia dell'arte*. Unlike those of Molière, the useless-precaution plays of Fatouville and Regnard show that these two writers never outgrew the use of the Italian character types. But let us return now to Spain where, as in the *enxemplos* (I shall prefer this old-Spanish variant spelling from now on), the first cuckold works depict a husband, for he did not become a guardian until the time of Molière.

FIRST SPANISH ARTISTIC DEVELOPMENTS OF THE THEME: DECEIVED HUSBANDS AND DECEIVED BROTHERS

I. Cervantes' *Cueva de Salamanca*.

This *entremés* was written about 1611 but not published until 1615 in the collection *Ocho comedias y ocho entremeses nuevos nunca representados*. Pancracio informs his wife Leonarda that he must be away from home for four or five days. She feigns extreme sorrow, but as soon as he has gone she and her servant Cristina joyfully prepare a feast with victuals sent by the sacristan and barber who are to join them that night. Previous to their arrival, a poor student knocks and asks to spend the night in the straw loft. Permission is granted and leftovers from the meal are promised, with the student expected to earn his keep by helping pluck the fowls. The two guests arrive chagrined to find the student there. Although they would be rid of him, he remains. In the meantime a broken wheel on his carriage causes the husband to return unexpectedly during the banquet. The men hurry up to the loft while the wife receives her husband. Suddenly the student emerges from the loft shouting and choking. It is not difficult for the wife to explain his presence. The clever student then tells the husband about his abilities at magic learned in the cave of Salamanca. The curious husband is astonished when the student conjures up for him two demons in human form as well as a hamper of foods; and in order not to make the spirits too terrifying, the student causes the two phantoms to appear in the persons of the parish sacristan and Nicolás the barber. The husband accepts them as phantoms, and the skit ends as the party continues.

This slapstick piece is obviously a crude early form of our theme, but the invention of a phantom in order to avoid being caught will appear again in Dorimond's *La femme industrieuse* (1661). As in the *enxemplo* XCI from Sánchez de Vercial, Cervantes has the husband going out on the road, the hiding of the lover(s), the feast, and the wife's being assisted in the affair by another female. It is similar also to another *enxemplo*, XC, of the same collection: When a husband goes out to reap, his wife thinks he will be gone sufficiently long to allow her to receive her lover, so she prepares a fine repast. The husband injures an eye, returns, and lets his wife medicate preventively the good eye while, with the husband momentarily unable to see from either eye, the lover comes out of hiding and makes an escape.

Another possible source is the Fifth Day, Tenth Story, in Boccaccio's *Decameron*. Here the gallant, whose counterpart in Cervantes would have to be the student, is hidden under a pallet in a hen-coop whence, after preparations for a meal and the sudden return of the husband, he emerges roaring when stepped on, first having aroused the husband's suspicions by a series of inadvertent sneezes. Predating Boccaccio, however, the hen-coop tale had a derivative in *Calila y Dimna*.

II. Cervantes' *El viejo celoso*.

Among the same *ocho entremeses* is the one entitled *El viejo celoso*, a title which appears in one of the *commedia dell'arte* scenarios called *Il vecchio geloso*. It is still doubtful whether Cervantes wrote this *entremés* before or after *El celoso extremeño*, one of the *Novelas ejemplares* published in 1613.[7] Since *El celoso extremeño* seems to be an enlargement of *El viejo celoso*, one might judge the latter to have been written first and label it c. 1612. The point is moot but not of great importance to this study.

El viejo celoso and *El celoso extremeño* are among the first works to emphasize the details of the useless precaution. In the

---

[7] The controversy regarding this chronology is summarized in footnote three of S. Griswold Morley, *The Interludes of Cervantes* (Princeton, 1948), p. viii of the preface.

former, the 70-year-old rich husband is married to a poor girl of 15, an age relationship that was to become the norm in later workings of the theme. Here the jealous old man nails the windows, locks the doors, watches the house every moment, drives away tomcats and male dogs, and refuses to buy a tapestry with human figures. Seven doors, besides the door onto the street, lead to the wife's room. Each door has a lock and key. The husband hides the keys, patrols the house at night, and throws stones at serenaders or other groups in the street.

In the *enxemplo* XCI, derived from the *Disciplina Clericalis*, the wife and mother hold the ends of a *lienzo* to shield the escape of the lover, a common device of frequent use in Spanish Renaissance literature. In *El viejo celoso*, the wife Lorenza aided by her neighbor Hortigosa hold up a tapestry for the husband Cañizares to judge while the gallant sneaks behind it into the house. The device is the same; the direction of the gallant's movement is reversed. Later the gallant escapes as Lorenza dashes a basin of water in her husband's eyes and upbraids him for his suspicions. All the noise brings Hortigosa and a constable. The ironic ending has Cañizares begging the pardon of the go-between Hortigosa. It is the arrival of the constable, however, which is important as the first use of an appurtenance to the theme which found its way into the considerably later useless-precaution works of Sedaine and Beaumarchais.

Three important contributions to the theme, therefore, emerge from Cervantes' *El viejo celoso*:

(1) an emphasis upon the greatly disparate age relationship between the cuckold and the girl (though the old-young aspect does appear in Jacques de Vitry, *Calila y Dimna*, and certain Eastern works);

(2) the precautionary details of guarding the house; and

(3) the arrival of the police at the end.

III. CERVANTES' *El celoso extremeño*.

It is noteworthy that in this *novela ejemplar*, dated 1613, the ages of the jealous husband and of his young wife, 70 and 15 respectively, are identical to those of the same pair in *El viejo celoso*, as are their respective stations of rich and poor. Here, however, for the first time, is the simple wife, so innocent that she dressed dolls and had other childish pastimes. Here too are not only the details of how Carrizales guards the house, but in addition those of its special construction and outfitting in accordance with Carrizales' obsession that Leonora shall not have any contact with the world. Despite their similar age and station, Carrizales of *El celoso extremeño* and Cañizares of the previous work differ in that Carrizales is likable and kind, and at the end he is to be pitied; moreover, his young wife is not really discontented and is genuinely fond of him. Thus Cervantes tends to utilize the cuckold theme here as a vehicle for demonstrating one of his recurring apprehensions: the misfortunes that can be caused by a corrupt *dueña*. She of course is the go-between.

It has been stated that the unifying aspect of all variations of this theme—ones that are more than anecdotes like the *enxemplos*—is the intrigue for the gallant to enter the house. Here for the first time this intrigue is embellished with full details of the gallant's stratagems, which succeed only after careful planning and repeated assaults. This might indicate that more than one subsequent version of the theme was written by an author who knew the work by Cervantes, or who knew a previous work in turn inspired in Cervantes (or in Lope de Vega, as we shall see), because most of the acting time in the *Barber of Seville*, for example, is given to experimentation with the successive Figaro-inspired plans to introduce the Count into the house.

Loaysa disguises himself as a lame beggar and very gradually ingratiates himself first with the Negro doorkeeper Luis and then with the *dueña* and the other servants, all by reason of his ability to sing and play the guitar. It is through the use of pincers, hammer, and a wax key that Loaysa at last enters the innermost rooms of the house. Even Leonora finally is entranced by his dulcet guitar. This proves to be her downfall when Carrizales discovers Leonora and Loaysa closeted together. Although Leonora is innocent of that which Carrizales takes for granted as he finds the pair asleep together, her sincere grief cannot prevent his resultant quick decline and death. The notary arrives to make the will. One week later, Leonora, although generously provided for, has chosen to become a nun; Loaysa, who had hoped to marry her, goes to the Indies; the domestics are compensated and freed; Leonora's parents are grieved but consoled with their new wealth; and only the bad *dueña* is left in poverty.

In a short literary study on the origin of *El celoso extremeño*,[8] Angel González Palencia reviews certain sources that have been suggested.[9] He does not lend much credence—nor do I—to the claim for the Italian ones offered (Sercambi, Cieco de Ferrara, Boiardo, Straparola, and others)[10] nor to Rodríguez Marín's theory that the models of *El celoso extremeño* were taken from real life. He mentions the *Disciplina Clericalis* and the *Libro de los enxemplos*, specifically not only *enxemplo* XCI, which we have discussed already in connection with *El viejo celoso*, but also *enxemplo* CCXXXV.[11]

In *enxemplo* CCXXXV a man asks advice on how best to guard a wife. He is advised to put his wife in a tall house with stone walls, with openings limited to one door for passage and one window. The house having been built and the domestic routine established, he sleeps with the door key under his head. One day the wife sees a gallant through the window, consorts with him, and then night after night plies her husband with excessive wine so that he might not notice her likewise-nightly excursions to meet the gallant. The husband becomes suspicious, and the remaining events of his locking her out, her pretended jump into the well (it was a stone she had dropped), his going to the well while she sneaks back into the house, her locking him out thus to deny to her relatives (previously summoned by the husband) the truth of his accusations—all are derived from the *Disciplina Clericalis* and

---

[8] This study by Angel González Palencia was published originally in *Homenaje a Menéndez Pidal*, I (Madrid, 1924), 417-423, under the title "Un cuento popular marroquí y *El celoso extremeño*, de Cervantes." I have used and shall refer to the following reprinting of the same material: ANGEL GONZÁLEZ PALENCIA, "El celoso engañado," *Historias y leyendas* (Madrid, 1942), pp. 163-173.

[9] He discusses these studies: F. RODRÍGUEZ MARÍN, *El Loaysa de El celoso extremeño* (Seville, 1901); E. MELE, "La novella *El celoso extremeño*," *Nuova antologia*, CXXV (1906), p. 475; M. A. GARRONE, "*El celoso extremeño*, de Cervantes, y una novela de G. F. Straparola," *España moderna*, II (1910), p. 158; and R. SCHEVILL and A. BONILLA's edition of the *Obras* of Cervantes, VI of the *Comedias y entremeses*, p. 107 ff.

[10] For further commentary on these proposed Italian sources, as well as other possible sources, see Cirot, *op. cit.*, p. 6 ff.

[11] See p. 505 of the same reference in fn. 3.

reappear in the Seventh Day, Fourth Story, of Boccaccio's *Decameron*, which probably gave Molière the idea for similar events in *La jalousie du barbouillé*. It is in this *enxemplo* CCXXXV that one finds the first details of house-guarding on the part of the husband. This means it is probably the earliest Spanish manifestation of the precautionary aspect of the theme of the cuckold, an aspect lacking in the aforementioned *enxemplo* XCI and one which Cervantes was the first to exploit fully in both *El viejo celoso* and *El celoso extremeño*.

The main part of González Palencia's study is his narration of a Moroccan folk tale. He reproduces it in Spanish but claims to have heard the original Arabic in Rabat in 1914 from the lips of one Mohámed Belhach, a young mail clerk who knew no European language at all. The tale goes as follows:

A man whose previous wives had deceived him buys a baby girl, having promised her mother to care for the girl and take her to wife when she has become a woman. He rears the girl to believe that "...*en el mundo no hay más que yo, tú y Dios*" (p. 164). One day when the "father" goes out, an old mendicant woman comes to the door to beg. The girl, surprised to find there are other people in the world, is even more anxious to see the fine young man whom the old woman proposes to bring to her. The beggar advises the girl to grease her face with a yellow substance, retire to her bed, feign illness, and inform her guardian that she, the old beggar, knows the illness and can treat it. The plan succeeds, and the guardian allows the woman to go for her trunk of medicines. Naturally a gallant is in the trunk. The unsuspecting guardian must agree to leave the house for a week to allow the old woman time to work her medicines. He returns after the week to find the girl "well," but when porters drop the trunk as they haul it outside, it breaks open and the gallant is discovered. The ending has the guardian go insane, after having first pardoned the girl and deeded all his properties to her. She remains in the house to enjoy the fortune with the gallant and the old woman; but finally, everything spent, she too is reduced to begging alms in the streets.

Certain similarities to Cervantes' *El celoso extremeño* are obvious: the jealous husband, the simple wife who is a victim of others' deceits, her humble origin, her cloisture, the precautions, the immoral *tercera*, the intrigue to gain admittance to the house, the use of an ointment, the girl's parent (in Cervantes, parents) in person, and the girl's being pardoned and receiving her sponsor's wealth. Could Cervantes have heard some story like this one during his long stay in Argel? *The Thousand and One Nights* does not contain any version of this story; but the admittedly undocumentable tale points to the Arabs, as does the *Disciplina Clericalis*, as the channel for introduction of the Cervantes-type cuckold theme into Spain.

Whatever their Eastern source, if any, these are the new adjuncts to the basic theme as propagated by *El celoso extremeño*:

(1) not in any of the *enxemplos*, but in the Arabic folk tale: the simple wife of humble origin, to be exploited in the Zayas-Scarron version of the theme and derived works like Dorimond's *L'école des cocus*, Molière's *L'école des femmes*, and others.

(2) the *details* of purchasing the house.

(3) the husband's travels before his decision to marry and lead a domestic life, or, the way this element developed sometimes in other versions, his leaving the house for some purpose—all with precedent in the *enxemplos* XC and XCI, as repeated in the oral Arabic tale, and also as having occurred in *La cueva de Salamanca*.

(4) the gallant's disguising himself to enter the house, the first *Spanish* manifestation of a long series of varying disguises in subsequent works; and the increased emphasis upon this intrigue to gain entry into the house.

(5) the bribe, here with music, for someone to gain entrance to the house.

(6) the appearance of the notary at the end. In certain later versions the notary makes an appearance at the end in order to marry the girl to her gallant.

(7) the precautionary (*précaution inutile*) aspect of the theme, either taken from or passed on to *El viejo celoso*, depending on which work was written first.

IV. More Deceived Husbands: María de Zayas y Sotomayor's *El prevenido, engañado* (1637 or earlier) [12] and Paul Scarron's *La précaution inutile* (1655). [13]

Scarron is usually credited with invention of the phrase *précaution inutile* which came to be bandied about somewhat loosely in variations of the theme subsequent to his. Because the words *précaution inutile* did gain wide currency as a set phrase in cuckold works, their use in a title or subtitle does not reliably indicate the derivation of its plot. More than one writer has been deceived in this matter through not realizing how many *précaution inutile* plays there were in seventeenth- and eighteenth-century France. For example, Florence N. Jones concludes (*op. cit.*, p. 16) that Fatouville's *La précaution inutile* (1692) was for *Le barbier de Séville* "a source which would seem to be plainly indicated by the subtitle of the *Barbier*." Using the same reasoning, Professor Edwin Place relates the *Barbier* not to Fatouville but to Scarron when he says that "of course, the subtitle of Beaumarchais' play is here the clincher, leading straight back to Scarron and Zayas." [14] Thus Dr. Place contends [15] that a work so late as Beaumarchais' *Barbier de Séville* (1775) is traceable to Scarron mainly because *La précaution inutile* was both the subtitle of Beaumarchais' play and also the name of an air sung by Rosine under the tutelage of Count Almaviva when he is disguised as a music teacher. [16] It seems inconceivable that critics like Brunetière, Lanson, Lintilhac, Morillot, Chardon, Fitzmaurice-Kelly, *et al.* could have propagated, as they did, any Scarron-Beaumarchais relationship other than the broad sameness of theme apparent in all cuckold works. Rather, as we have

---

[12] Available in various editions. The text used was in this edition of her stories: *Novelas amorosas y ejemplares* (Barcelona, 1646), pp. 86-119, a copy of which is owned by the University of Chicago library.

[13] Available in *Oeuvres de Scarron*, tome troisième (Paris, 1786), 233-280.

[14] Edwin B. Place, "Beaumarchais and Bibliography," *The French Review*, Vol. XXIX, No. 1 (Oct., 1955), p. 58.

[15] Edwin B. Place, "María de Zayas, an Outstanding Woman Short-Story Writer of Seventeenth Century Spain," *University of Colorado Studies*, Vol. XIII (June, 1923), p. 22.

[16] It is irrelevant but noteworthy that in his opera, which otherwise follows the *Barbier de Séville* quite closely, Rossini did not consider it important to have a useless-precaution aria for the occasion of the music lesson. Instead he calls for an *ad libitum* air at the discretion of the troupe.

just seen, the precautionary aspect of the theme evolves from Cervantes' *El viejo celoso* and *El celoso extremeño,* where, beyond the mere concept of cuckolding a husband, there are elaborated for the first time the details of the husband's measures to keep his wife incommunicada from the world. Maybe the phrase *précaution inutile* originated with Scarron, but the idea of the useless precaution, the simple wife, and other details came from Cervantes or the *enxemplos,* and was seized upon by María de Zayas, of whose work Scarron's is merely an unacknowledged translation.

El prevenido, engañado is the story of one Don Fadrique's travails with the deceits of women. Briefly his experiences may be grouped into five episodes. A separate woman figures in each episode. First he is duped by Serafina, who, secretly to all but Fadrique, bears and abandons another's baby, which Fadrique is kind enough to place in a convent. In Seville he is deluded next by Beatriz, who, Fadrique discovers, has a secret passion for a Negro in her employ. In Madrid Fadrique is deceived by Violante. Then he leaves Spain and travels abroad for sixteen years. After he has returned to Spain, it happens that he passes a castle and strikes up an acquaintanceship with the duchess of that castle. By now very much *escarmentado,* he confesses to her that he is seeking a wife who is a simpleton. In the fifth and last episode, and after he has had amusing experiences at the expense of the duchess' husband, Fadrique decides to establish a home by taking from the convent and marrying none other than Gracia, the illegitimate daughter of the earlier Serafina.

This fifth episode is the one relevant to our topic and the one of which it is claimed that "the well-known *Barbier de Séville* is an imitation."[17] Here, as part of his precautionary measures, the jealous husband has the simple wife stand guard at night, armed,[18] since "that is what married people do." A *galán* instructs her other-

---

[17] Place, p. 21 of the *op. cit.* in fn. 15.
[18] Professor Place, *op. cit.* in fn. 15, has traced this odd element to an Italian source, though it occurred also in the *Cent Nouvelles Nouvelles.* The device of the armor is probably a main Zayas contribution to the theme in the French language, through either Scarron's *Précaution inutile* or d'Ouville's acknowledged translation of Zayas' story. This single episode is the basis of *L'école des cocus* by Dorimond, who also used the armed-guard idea in *La femme industrieuse.*

wise when the husband leaves on a business trip. The moral is that simple wives are no safer than scheming ones, who at least know enough to conceal their indiscretions. This is not at all the point of Beaumarchais' *Barbier de Séville* nor of Cervantes' *El celoso extremeño*, both of which truly emphasize the *précaution inutile* against the gallant's many schemes for entering the house. Once the gallant has attained his goal, the Zayas and Cervantes works have much the same ending. After the death of the husband in *El prevenido, engañado*, the innocent wife and her mother have a handsome inheritance and enter a convent. This is precisely the situation of Leonora at the end of *El celoso extremeño*, where the parents get the money and she goes to the convent alone.

Although both Professors Place (see fn. 15) and Sylvania [19] in their respective articles of 1923 spoke of Zayas' conceivable indebtedness to Cervantes' *El casamiento engañoso* for her tale *El castigo de la miseria*, neither mentioned the obvious likeness between *El prevenido, engañado* and Cervantes' *El celoso extremeño*, to which the former bears much greater similarity than any to the *Barbier de Séville*. Here are some points of comparison between *El prevenido, engañado* and *El celoso extremeño*, features not present in the *Barbier de Séville*:

(1) the husband's *nobleza* and *riqueza* and his having *corrido mucho mundo* because his parents had died early in his life;

(2) the husband's intent to overcome difficulties with wealth and his supposed knowledge of the wiles of the world;

(3) the male Negro servant;

(4) the *tercera*;

(5) the would-be husband's speaking to a girl's parents to ask for her hand;

(6) Fadrique's sixteen-year absence and Carrizales' twenty-year absence before their return to their own land to marry;

(7) the handpicked wife, servants, and accessories to the project of obtaining and keeping a young and simple wife; and

(8) the aforementioned ending in the nunnery after the death of the jealous husband. The main difference between the fifth episode of *El prevenido, engañado* and *El celoso extremeño* is also the

---

[19] E. V. SYLVANIA, "Doña María de Zayas y Sotomayor: A Contribution to the Study of Her Works," *Romanic Review*, XIV (1923), 199-232.

principal likeness between the latter and the *Barbier de Séville*, indeed the whole basis of action: the long and difficult intrigue to gain admittance to the house (note: both in Seville, not Granada as in Zayas), a process which in Zayas was relatively easy. This zest for the quest and its dependent framework of detailed and repeated stratagems to gain entrance, stemming from Cervantes, was to become the essence of the theme. The Zayas-Scarron main contribution to the theme is the variant element that a simple wife is no guarantee against the cuckolding of a jealous husband. This moral was to be exploited more elaborately by Molière in *L'école des femmes*, vulgarized by Dorimond in *L'école des cocus*, and recalled in other post Dorimond-Molière works.

V. NEW TACK: THE BROTHER-GUARDIAN PLAYS: LOPE DE VEGA'S *El mayor imposible* (presented 1615, published 1647) [20] and derived works: FRANÇOIS LE METEL DE BOIS-ROBERT'S *La folle gageure* (1653) [21]; AGUSTÍN MORETO'S *No puede ser el guardar una mujer* (1661); NOLANT DE FATOUVILLE'S (attributed to him) *La précaution inutile* (1692). [22]

Comparative dates shows Cervantes' *Cueva de Salamanca* (c. 1611), *El viejo celoso* (c. 1612), and *El celoso extremeño* (1613) all to have preceded Lope's *El mayor imposible* (1615) by a few years. The theme takes a new bent with Lope's play, which was to have a progeny in both Spanish and French literature. Lope too fashions his plot with schemes for the gallant to penetrate the house, but the deceived tyrant is the girl's brother rather than her husband or tutor.

Lope's play has a background of fictitious history set in Italy. Queen Antonia, who is holding an *academia*, argues with Roberto in Act I as follows:

---

[20] Has been edited by John Brooks, complete text and notes in *University of Arizona Bulletin*, Vol. V, No. 7 (October 1, 1934).
[21] A 1653 Paris edition was the one used in this study. In the U.S.A., these university libraries have copies of the play: Princeton, Cornell, Johns Hopkins, Chicago, Kansas, and California (Berkeley).
[22] Available in *Théâtre italien*, tome I, Paris, n.d.

> Roberto, si una mujer
> quiere, yo tengo por cierto
> que es imposible guardarla.

When Roberto disagrees with this opinion, the Queen secretly orders Lisardo to conquer Roberto's own sister, Diana. At home the brother orders his servant Fulgencio, the *viejo*, not to permit any male being, even servants, to enter the house or speak to Diana. Ramón, who is Lisardo's servant and the *gracioso*, suggests to the Queen, naturally in return for a promised monetary reward, a plan whereby he will enter the house in order subsequently to open it to Lisardo. (In the meantime, Roberto has discovered a picture of Lisardo smuggled to Diana.) Ramón poses as a certain Don Pedro in the service of an admiral who is a friend of Roberto. The false Pedro calls at the home of Roberto with six fine horses (supplied by the Queen) supposedly a gift from the admiral. When "Pedro" presents also a (forged) written request that he be retained to tend the horses, the unsuspecting Roberto obligingly invites him into the house. In a note from Lisardo, Diana learns the truth about "Pedro" and the horses.

Ramón arranges with Diana that Lisardo shall enter the garden that night dressed as a porter who is to bring a trunk of "Pedro's" clothes into the house. Fulgencio supervises this action by order of Roberto, but only the second bearer is seen to enter and leave, and Lisardo remains in the house. (Cf. Cervantes' *El viejo celoso* in which the gallant slips by unseen when the tapestry is raised.) Act II ends as Diana and Lisardo meet in the garden, she agreeing to hide him for the night as follows:

> Un oratorio cae
> junto a mi cama, y en él
> serás esta noche imagen.

As Act III begins, we learn that Lisardo has been hidden not one night but seven. When the servants finally become suspicious, Lisardo forces his way out of the house. Roberto, furious, goes to see the Queen, to whom he must concede that guarding a woman is harder than he had thought. When he indicates his intention to cloister Diana in a nunnery, the Queen passes this information to Lisardo. The latter, again with the aid of Ramón, manages to extricate Diana from the house before Roberto can take any further steps.

In the end, all come before the King and Queen (the King and the real admiral have just returned) where everything is explained to Roberto. At first he demands a duel but is satisfied when Lisardo explains that no one's honor was sullied and that he and Diana are now truly in love and wish to marry. The precautions were useless, but all turns out well. Even Ramón marries Diana's servant, Celia.

The editor, John Brooks (see fn. 20), suggests as a possible source for the play the situation of Ovid's story of Danaë, whose variations gave Lope plots for more than one play. However this may be, the whole plane of action in *El mayor imposible* differs greatly from anything in Cervantes and the Cervantes-types, yet it has all the basic elements of the useless-precaution theme as well as some of the variant ones: the woman impossible to guard; the deceived protector; the go-between (whose resourcefulness is worthy of a Figaro); the same valet's bribe to action; the disguise for entering the house; the secret communication (here the portrait and the note) between girl and gallant; and the tyrant's precautions.

Whenever the guardian and girl are brother and sister in subsequent useless-precaution plays, it may be assumed that the work in question stems from either Lope or a Lope-derivative.

Chronologically the first imitation of Lope's brother-sister play was a French one: Bois-Robert's *La folle gageure, ou Les divertissements de la Comtesse de Pembroc* (1653). In a preface to the reader, Bois-Robert admits having reworked Lope's play, which in general he follows closely despite modification of some details. [23] He retains only one name from Lope's list of characters, that of Diane (Diana). He changes the setting from Italy to London. Instead of a queen we have a countess as mediator, but the main innovation is the bet.

It is an innovation in little more than name only. The forces within and without the house in most versions of the theme seem

---

[23] For a scene-by-scene running comparison of the two plays, see WILLIAM H. BOHNING, "Lope's *El mayor imposible* and Boisrobert's *La folle gageure*," *Hispanic Review*, XII (1944), 248-257.

to operate within the spirit of a challenge; if unwritten and unstated, then certainly it is a mutually understood wager or contest. Bois-Robert merely formalized an existing situation with the apt label of "foolish bet." Probably thus he intended to sharpen the outline of Lope's basic plot, though a bet can contribute but little suspense to a foregone conclusion.

The wager is between Telame (the brother) and Lidamont (the gallant) concerning, of course, whether or not Diane can be guarded successfully. Lidamont and his valet Philipin plan their campaign with mostly the same stratagems already described from Lope's play, including the gift of the six horses. Assuredly Telame loses the bet, but he accepts defeat much more graciously than did Lope's deceived brother. Although the formalized bet conceivably gives an extra portion of unity to the plot, it remained for Moreto to recapture the sprightliness of Lope's play sans wager.

Agustín Moreto's *No puede ser* (1661) is another obvious recast of Lope's *El mayor imposible*. If Moreto knew Bois-Robert's play, he took nothing from it, unless it be the valet's disguise as a merchant; but, like Bois-Robert, he did change Lope's locale and modify some of the events. Most of the same characters reappear with different names.

This play too begins with an *academia,* led by an illustrious and learned lady of Madrid who, like Lope's Queen, instigates the deception of the brother. As usual, the schemes to enter the house are the mainstay of the action; but a deviation from Lope here has the servant Tarugo pose as an *indiano,* just arrived in Spain with a letter of introduction from a marquis in Mexico who is a friend of the brother. The device of the newly-arrived *indiano,* coupled with these lines referring to the brother:

> Con ella viene don Pedro
> Pacheco, nuestro vecino,
> que es un *Celoso extremeño*
> en el guardar a su hermana.

suggests that Moreto had borne Cervantes' work in mind even if Lope had not. Moreto's ending is like Lope's, at least the important part of it, having to do with the brother's enlightenment and the marriage of his sister to the gallant.

La précaution inutile (1692), attributed to Nolant (or variously spelled Noland or Nolent) de Fatouville, exhibits some elements derived from all three predecessors, as well as from Molière and possibly others; however, it has at least one element that, not employed in Bois-Robert, necessarily links Fatouville directly to a Spanish source. In the case of Fatouville one must reckon also with the influence of the Italian *commedia dell'arte*, because the works attributed to him are of the period when Parisian playwrights were imitating the technique of the Italian improvised plays; furthermore, Fatouville wrote exclusively for the Comédie Italienne. Although the basic plot is undoubtedly that of Lope, it is not impossible that the whole brother-guardian series, beginning with Lope, might have been suggested by some Italian scenario with a captain as the brother. This is just a suspicion; I have no evidence.

Not always is the Spanish parentage of Fatouville's *Précaution inutile* duly noted by those who have commented on the play. (Lancaster does note that its source is Lope.) [24] With regard to its imitations, Lintilhac says that, after Molière, Fatouville's play was the work that Beaumarchais imitated most for his *Barbier de Séville*. [25] L. de Loménie, one of Beaumarchais' biographers, doubts whether this imitation was direct. [26] Despite the comparative passages from the two plays which Lintilhac offers as proof of his statement (*loc. cit.*), and aside from the person of the amorous doctor, I fail to find anything but the scheme of a Lope-type in Fatouville and that of a Cervantes-type in Beaumarchais. The elements and sources of the *Barbier de Séville* will be discussed in more detail later, but by now it is hoped that the reader recognizes the two separate lines of development of the theme which will henceforth be labelled as Cervantes-type and Lope-type, such labelling not to imply necessarily that the author in question knew at first hand any Cervantes or Lope de Vega work.

---

[24] HENRY CARRINGTON LANCASTER, *A History of French Dramatic Literature in the Seventeenth Century, Part IV: The Period of Racine, 1673-1700*, Vol. II (Baltimore: London: Paris, 1940), p. 628.
[25] EUGÈNE LINTILHAC, *Histoire générale du théâtre en France*, Vol. IV (Paris, n.d.), p. 403.
[26] L. DE LOMÉNIE, *Beaumarchais et son temps*, Vol. I (Paris, 1880), p. 474.

Besides the academy-brother-sister elements and its other general characteristics which invite comparison with Lope, Fatouville's play is indeed interesting for its display of scattered interim (post-Lope to 1692) elements of the theme, including not only reflections of Molière but also its title *La précaution inutile* à la Scarron, and, in addition, its characters straight from the standardized names and types of the *commedia dell'arte*. Notwithstanding most critics' opinions to the contrary, this play is in my judgment a most entertaining farce, well constructed, but of course lacking the genius of character development through self-explanation which seemed to be Molière's special province. A detailed analysis of its plot is necessary for comparison not only with Lope, Bois-Robert, and Moreto, but also with types of the *commedia dell'arte* as well as with the useless-precaution works of Molière and Beaumarchais to be described later. At the same time, perhaps the reader can judge for himself what, if anything, there is of Fatouville in Beaumarchais other than the general sameness common to all workings of our theme. In my opinion, moreover, this is the one useless-precaution work most suitable to be described as typical of the whole genre.

The *dramatis personae* are stock names from the *commedia dell'arte*:

GAUFICHON:	Amant d'Isabelle
COLOMBINE:	Sœur de Gaufichon
MARINETTE:	Servante de Gaufichon
PASQUARIEL PIERROT	} Valets de Gaufichon
LÉANDRE:	Amant de Colombine
ISABELLE:	Cousine de Léandre
MEZZETIN ARLEQUIN	} Valets de Léandre
DOCTOR BALOUARD	

Lackeys, porters, tradesmen, coachmen, etc.

The *dottore* of the *commedia dell'arte* usually had the name of Dr. Gratiano or, as here, Dr. Balouard (in Italian, Dr. Baloardo). In the *commedia dell'arte* he was frequently the cuckold. Although in Fatouville's play the *dottore* shares in the duping, he is not its principal target. That is Gaufichon, the brother. Pasquariel, Pierrot, and Mezzetin are typical *valets intrigants*. The name Arlequin needs no introduction, nor do those of Colombine and Marinette. In other Italian-influenced works, Colombine usually has the role of a menial. Here she is the sister, maybe for a good reason: the most frequent name for the *amoureuse* and principal lady, Isabella or Isabelle, a name to occur with regularity in our useless-precaution plays, probably had to be given to Léandre's cousin in her capacity of overseer of the intrigue. The only thing lacking is a captain, but we shall see him in other useless-precaution works.

The setting is in Paris. Each of the four brother-sister plays thus is placed in a different locale: Italy, England, Spain, and France.

In the first scene, Gaufichon asks Colombine: "*Ma soeur, songez-vous que demain vous serez la femme d'un Docteur?*" It will be seen later that the notion of "marriage tomorrow" is a trace from Molière. The initial *académie* scenes take place in the rooms of Isabelle. When she, Colombine, and Léandre all agree how difficult it is to guard a woman who wills not to be guarded, Gaufichon becomes angry and declares that his sister shall indeed marry Doctor Balouard, who is also present. Léandre appeals to Isabelle for help, Gaufichon having made an exit declaring that "*...ma maison sera baricadée....*"

Like Bois-Robert's countess, but unlike her counterpart in Lope, Isabelle does not organize the campaign against Gaufichon. She merely lends support to the plans of Léandre and Mezzetin. Mezzetin declares confidently that *demain* Léandre shall be Colombine's husband.

The first of the deceits occurs in no other version of the theme that I have read. Arlequin has overheard Gaufichon say: "*...j'ay envoyé chercher un masson & un serrurier, pour faire boucher tous les endroits de ma maison par où l'on peut m'insulter.*" Mezzetin and Arlequin disguise themselves as mason and locksmith and receive from Gaufichon detailed instructions for the work required. They inform him, however, of a law that forbids workers to wall up women, and he foolishly feels it necessary to slip them a bribe. After they have left, Colombine tells Gaufichon of her resolve to defy him. She quotes from Molière: "*...avez-vous déja oublié les oracles de Moliere* (sic), *qui vous a dit si précisément*: 'Les verroux & les grilles ne font pas la vertu des femmes & des *filles.*'"At this point Pasquariel runs in to tell how he has just saved the life of a poor English merchant who was being pummeled.

This *marchand anglois* who takes refuge in Gaufichon's house is none other than Mezzetin in a new disguise, one reminiscent of the pretended diamond merchant in Bois-Robert, as well as the cloth merchant in Moreto. (A valet's disguise as a merchant will be seen again in Gueullette's *Le remède à la mode*.) Here is an interesting political note: Mezzetin explains that the fracas was caused by people who were trying to confiscate his merchandise, trade between France and England being prohibited at that time. When Colombine shows an interest in his merchandise (stockings), there arises the question of its authenticity "because of the war." Mezzetin hands to Colombine his supposed letter of authorized sales representation, which is really a love letter from Léandre assuring her of being delivered from both brother and doctor. Gaufichon grabs the note and reads it but does not know who wrote it, for it says that the bearer, who incidentally has made a hasty exit, will identify the author.

Again Gaufichon assures the amorous Dr. Balouard that he shall have Colombine *demain*, but at that moment Pasquariel announces the arrival of a water carrier at the door. It is Pierrot dressed in female attire. Among works of the theme, this disguise as a water carrier is exclusive to Fatouville's play, but in other uselessprecaution plays we shall see the guardian often disguised as a woman. A scuffle ensues in which the feigned *porteuse d'eau* drops a letter written by Colombine. The letter tells the recipient to carry forward without violence the intention announced in the letter received previously by Colombine. When Gaufichon calls her to task, Colombine invents an explanation: a certain Capitaine de Bombardiers named M. de Brise-roche has been bothering her with unwanted attentions; and, both pressed for an answer to his letter and also in order to calm him, she has written this note to avoid violence. The doctor and Gaufichon are deceived and agree even to let the letter be delivered. Naturally Gaufichon must give the water carrier more money.

The next of the comic deceptions is the arrival of a tailor, this time Arlequin in another disguise. Gaufichon admits him, because if Colombine is to be married tomorrow she must attend to her clothing. It is during this interview between Colombine and the feigned tailor that the latter gives her Léandre's portrait. The smuggling of the portrait to the sister originated in Lope and was perpetuated in Bois-Robert and Moreto before Fatouville. Here Colombine also sends her own portrait to Léandre by means of the "tailor," who is unaware that she had exchanged portraits.

As in previous versions, the brother finds the portrait of the gallant. Now Gaufichon borrows a cloak from Isabelle and disguises himself as a coachman among his servants to discover who had brought the portrait. It was of course a mistake to tell his plans to Isabelle, because she then causes Pierrot also to be disguised as a coachman. A number of funny scenes ensue, the upshot of which is the further burlesquing and fleecing of Gaufichon by his own servants. It is to be noted that the untrustworthy guards are a Molière element with precedent in the events of Cervantes' *El celoso extremeño*; in Lope, Bois-Robert, and Moreto the house is breached in spite of the guard rather than because of his disloyalty. When Gaufichon finally discards the unsuccessful disguise as coachman, he finds Colombine feigning to chastise her maid Marinette for having been negligent in the matter of the portrait, which supposedly the latter had found outside the house and should have returned to its owner. Arlequin substantiates this lie. Thus again Colombine deceives Gaufichon and evades his wrath.

The tricks continue. Now Arlequin is disguised as a country gentleman, the Baron de Fourbadiere, with Mezzetin as his valet. Supposedly Arlequin has been sent by a relative and bears a letter asking that Gaufichon please aid him in making purchases in Paris and lodge him at a good inn. Gaufichon with his *noblesse oblige* naturally insists that the "Baron" stay with him, and is not displeased when the pretended Baron says he cannot bear the sight of women and will accept the invitation only if the women of the house stay out of sight. This is precisely the situation in Lope when "Pedro," supposedly in the service of the admiral, brings the six horses. The interloper feigns an antipathy for women in order to be certain of receiving an invitation to stay in the house. Fatouville, then, must have studied either Lope's or Moreto's play, because even though Bois-Robert has an admiral's squire bring the same six horses, he does not give the squire an allergy to women.

Ensuing events become increasingly complicated after Léandre arrives disguised as both *crocheteur* and the second servant of the

"Baron." This mode of arrival in the house is a distinctly different one from that of the gallant in Lope and Moreto, where he enters unseen behind the visitor's trunk, or from Bois-Robert where he is actually in the trunk. In all deceived-brother versions the gallant and his lady meet in the garden. Additional comic effect is achieved here when the pretended Baron faints, having seen a woman in the garden, and has to be carried to bed.

Early in the third and final act, Gaufichon seeks witnesses for the marriage contract while the doctor goes for the notary. The appearance of the notary probably stems from his presence in Molière's *L'école des maris* and *L'école des femmes*, and is utilized again in the later *Barbier de Séville*. No notary appears in Lope, Bois-Robert, or Moreto. The nonsense is not yet over, however, for Mezzetin comes dressed as a countess invited to be a witness. When Gaufichon turns his head, Colombine takes the clothes of the "countess." Gaufichon now perceives Mezzetin as a lackey and believes his sister to be the countess. The notary too has sport with Gaufichon by insisting that he was called to draw up a will. Finally, with everyone gathered for the last scene, Colombine identifies herself; and beginning with the mason and locksmith episode, everything is explained to Gaufichon. The brother is simply astounded, but Dr. Balouard good-naturedly admits that he himself has been a fool. Only one wedding takes place, that of Colombine and Léandre, whereas in Lope, Bois-Robert, and Moreto, two pacts were sealed. The play ends with a little song preceded by a few words from Colombine directed against useless precautions.

Fatouville's play is one of pure farce and is not highly regarded by anybody, yet it is the liveliest of the brother-guardian series. Although the characters are only types, somehow they seem to come to life; and for a play of its kind with all the disguises, the action has a remarkably unfatiguing continuity. It is the prototype of the light cuckold comedy and is thus somewhat removed from the less boisterous *El mayor imposible* of Lope. Surely of all the deceived protectors who pass upon the scene in the theme of the useless precaution, none is busier nor more frustrated and bilked than Fatouville's poor Gaufichon.

Apparently Fatouville traced his plot outline from Lope and embellished it with extraneous details both of his own invention as well as from other sources. Then he immersed the whole product into an atmosphere of *commedia dell'arte*. Whatever deviating elements that Moreto, Bois-Robert, and Fatouville introduced—all three plays had some new features—each one of these authors used certain other elements traceable, at the respective dates of publication, only to Lope. Therefore the deceived-brother plays all have something Spanish in origin.

DORIMOND. MOLIÈRE: DECEIVED GUARDIANS

Dorimond. Molière: the Guardian-and-Ward Plays:
(1) *L'école des maris* (première June 24, 1661);
(2) *L'école des femmes* (première December 26, 1662);
(3) *Le sicilien, ou L'amour peintre* (première February 9 or 10, 1667) and their antecedents.

The identical and then-novel feature among Molière's three useless-precaution plays is his causing the deceived tyrant to be not husband nor brother of the girl, but her guardian. The guardian in both *L'école des maris* and *L'école des femmes* spurs his opposition to quick action when he announces an intention to marry his ward "tomorrow." The (1) tutor-ward relationship and (2) decision to marry without delay are Molière's principal addition to the mechanics of the theme. They demonstrate his influence upon the post-Molière theater, in which they form the nucleus of the plot in nearly every later useless-precaution play. These two elements are transmitted to a work even as late as Beaumarchais' *Barbier de Séville* (1775), a play which, aside from this aspect of the plot that makes Molière's Sganarelle (*L'école des maris*) and Beaumarchais' Bartholo seem one and the same, is neither directly nor primarily derived from Molière. Therefore it will be easy to identify Molière-influenced useless-precaution works, but Molière's own sources present a problem. Even though his girl-tyrant relationship is neither Cervantes-descended (husband) nor Lope-descended (brother), some of Molière's other features surely are of the Cervantes-type. Nor should it go unobserved that Molière began his career under influence of the *commedia dell'arte* in Paris. For example, as his art developed, Molière allowed Sganarelle to become a flexible type, but originally this name was passed down from the role of the villain in the scenarios of the *commedia dell'arte*.

I. *L'école des maris.*

Opinion differs widely on the sources of both *L'école des maris* and *L'école des femmes*. Sleuths of the literary Scotland Yard have found this to be one of their most fascinating cases.[27] All or parts of each of the following five plays or play-groups have been proposed as sources for *L'école des maris*:

1. The Device of the Two Brothers. Near unanimity of agreement says that Terence's *Adelphi* is the earliest form of a similar situation in *L'école des maris*. In Terence, two brothers with opposite notions on life guide each of two young men in a different way. In Molière, it is each of two young women who are treated oppositely by the two brothers Sganarelle and Ariste. An intervenient form of this plot is Hurtado de Mendoza's *El marido hace mujer* (1643), in which two brothers differ in the amount and kind of liberty accorded their wives. Because this is the same idea as in Molière, except that Molière's women are not yet married, it led

---

[27] Even the standard histories of French and Spanish literature differ in this matter. For a more specialized sampling of these divergent and sometimes invective opinions, see the appropriate sections in the following works chosen at random:

    1. GUILLAUME HUSZÁR, *Molière et L'Espagne* (Paris, 1907).
    2. ERNEST MARTINECHE, "Les sources de *L'école des maris*," *Revue d'histoire littéraire de la France*, V (Jan. 15, 1898).
    3. ERNEST MARTINECHE, *La comédie espagnole en France de Hardy à Racine* (Paris, 1900).
    4. ERNEST MARTINECHE, *Molière et le théâtre espagnol* (Paris, 1906).
    5. EUGÈNE LINTILHAC, *Histoire générale du théâtre en France*, Vol. III (Paris, n.d.).
    6. S. GRISWOLD MORLEY, *Spanish Influence on Molière* (doctoral dissertation, Harvard, 1902).
    7. RAMÓN MESONERO ROMANOS, preliminary commentary to the edition of Antonio Hurtado de Mendoza's *El marido hace mujer y el trato muda costumbre*, in *Biblioteca de autores españoles*, Vol. XXXXV.
    8. A. PUIBUSQUE, *Histoire comparée des littératures espagnoles et françaises* (Paris, 1843).
    9. LANCASTER, *op. cit.*, Part III, *The Period of Molière, 1652-1672*, Vol. I (Baltimore: London: Paris, 1936).

Mesonero Romanos to argue that in *El marido hace mujer* "...no sólo es idéntico [i. e., to *L'école des maris*] el argumento, destinado a probar que la templanza y el cariño pueden más con la mujer que el rigor y los celos, sino que también presentado del mismo modo, con el ejemplo de los hermanos de opuestos caracteres, con casi idénticas situaciones, con la misma economía de acción, con las propias ideas y razonamientos, y hasta con la coincidencia del nombre de una de las damas [Leonor]."²⁸ Lancaster too believes this play to be a prime source for Molière.²⁹ We shall see presently that another contrast of husbands was available to Molière in Dorimond's *L'école des cocus*, although in Dorimond the two husbands are not brothers.

Be this as it may, Hurtado de Mendoza's play is a rather dull one compared with Molière's and not strictly within the general framework of the useless-precaution tradition, which, except in Lope-types, has the elderly guardian training his ward to his ways, or the elderly husband who believes he has trained his ward sufficiently before his marriage to her. The two brothers of Hurtado's play, who seem too young anyhow to qualify as traditional cuckolds, have just married two sisters who were neither wards nor "in training." The moral and title of Hurtado's play are in the Spanish tradition: wives are what husbands make them. The husband's authority is unchallenged; what is challenged is the husband's poor psychology. Molière's play, on the contrary, appears to be directed against undue male domestic authority regardless of how that authority is administered. In the long history of the useless-precaution theme, Molière was the first to speak out for women's rights *per se*, to delimit male authority rather than build a case, like Hurtado, upon the proper mode of exercising an *unquestioned* male authority.

2. Calderón de la Barca: *Guárdate del agua mansa*. The connection seems far fetched. Numerous Spanish plays like this one have an elderly father who closely supervises his daughter(s) while with parental prerogative he arranges a marriage for them. In the final analysis the daughter(s) manage to attract the man of their choice, who has perhaps had to conceal himself either in or out of

---

[28] Mesonero Romanos, *op. cit.* in fn. 27, p. xxx.
[29] Lancaster, *op. cit.* in fn. 27, I, 234-237.

the house, a situation which nearly always involves an exchange of secret notes.

3. Lope de Vega: *El mayor imposible*; Bois-Robert: *La folle gageure*; Moreto: *No puede ser*. We have already discussed these as a different branch of the same tree.

4. Lope de Vega: *La discreta enamorada* and/or the Third Day, Third Story, of the *Decameron*, itself probably Lope's source.[30] In Lope's play a young girl feigns to accept an old captain to whom she is promised in marriage. She is really in love with his son, against whom she invents untrue complaints that he is attempting to woo her with notes and vigils under her balcony. In this manner she conveys her real desires to the son, who at first had not understood his father's reprimand. Now the son's servant does in fact take him to see the girl. He becomes enamored of her and ultimately marries her after they have overcome obstacles in the persons of the girl's mother and the boy's father. The similarity among the three works (Boccaccio, Lope, Molière) lies, of course, in the girl's fictitious unwanted attentions, and the use of someone as an unsuspecting go-between (in the *Decameron*, a father-confessor; in Lope, the captain; in Molière, Sganarelle) for her and her gallant. The case for *La discreta enamorada* as a partial source work seems plausible.

Lope's play, however, is not really a useless-precaution work, for its remaining characteristics do not fit into the pattern of our theme any more than do those of certain devices for deceiving men in Lope's *Llegar en ocasión* and *El ruiseñor de Sevilla*, which by the way are plays also of possible origin in Boccaccio: Second Day, Second Story; and Fifth Day, Fourth Story, respectively. The wiles of a woman determined to marry her chosen lover are common enough in drama of the *Siglo de Oro*, but excepting Lope's *El mayor imposible*, such plays lack the most vital part of our theme: that of the sentinel and his preventive measures against any gallant's penetrating his domicile.

---

[30] See C. B. BOURLAND, "Boccaccio and the *Decameron* in Castilian and Catalan Literature," *Revue Hispanique*, XII (1905), 1-232.

5. Dorimond. *La femme industrieuse* [31] by Dorimond is in the vein of Lope's *Discreta enamorada* and has, moreover, the elements of the sentinel and the useless precautions that were lacking in Lope. The *privilège* of *La femme industrieuse* is dated March 26, 1661, preceding by three months the first performance of *L'école des maris* on June 24, 1661. Lancaster says that "there can be no doubt about the fact that Molière utilized Dorimond's *Femme industrieuse* or its sources in Boccaccio. It is possible that he went directly to the *Decameron*, but, as Dorimond had given the story dramatic form, had secularized the priest, and had been recently acting in Paris when Molière wrote it, it is more likely that he supplied the French dramatist with the material he had himself taken from Boccaccio." [32] Is it not true, however, that Lope had also secularized the priest?

Dorimond's *Femme industrieuse* merits close examination not only possibly as Molière's chief source, but also because its older elements of the theme are interestingly blended with innovations and enacted by character types from the *commedia dell'arte*.

The locale is Paris. Isabelle is the guarded yet neglected wife of a military man, a captain who at the outset leaves his valet Trapolin in charge of Isabelle while he goes off to amuse himself with other women. Of all the useless-precaution plays, this is the first in which the tyrant-husband is a philanderer. Isabelle, however, is not of the submissive or simple stamp of some of her predecessors. She fancies a certain Léandre and is determined to attract him during the captain's absence. Her method is precisely that of Lope and Boccaccio: by suggestion to a third party.

Trapolin, armed, escorts Isabelle to see a *docteur*, tutor of Léandre. She tells the tutor about unsolicited attentions on the part of his pupil. The tutor is impressed by her virtue and later scolds the surprised Léandre. His curiosity and libido now awakened, the libertine Léandre goes to address amorous words to Isabelle at her window, ill-guarded by the armed sentinel Trapolin. (Following this scene is a coarse one between Léandre and a certain Colinette.)

---

[31] A 1662 edition was the one used; a photostatic copy is available from the Johns Hopkins University library.
[32] LANCASTER, *op. cit.* in fn. 27, Vol. I, p. 235.

With new complaints, Isabelle pays more visits to the tutor. With each scolding, Léandre learns how to make new progress. Finally Isabelle complains that Léandre knew her husband was out of the house on a trip to the country, and that Léandre scaled the garden wall and silently slipped into her bedroom. After the usual scolding from his tutor, Léandre recognizes these to be his instructions and carries them out. He and Isabelle are surprised in the bedroom, however, when the captain returns "from the war of Coquetry" in good spirits and flushed with victory. The captain finds Isabelle's door locked and demands she open it. Léandre has a plan: he emerges dressed as a phantom. It is the spirit, he says, of a relative of Isabelle who has been protecting her virtue during her husband's absence. Trapolin is frightened; but the captain, on learning from the *phantosme* that Isabelle's high virtue makes guarding unnecessary, embraces the spirit and swears he will no longer guard her. Finis.

The main stratagem, encouragement by feigned accusation, obviously is derived from either Lope or Boccaccio. Probably from Zayas-Scarron comes the device of the armor. Here it is only the valet who wears the armor, but in Dorimond's *L'école des cocus* we shall see that it is the wife who wears it, as in Zayas-Scarron. The husband's absenting himself or taking a trip dates back through Zayas-Scarron to the *enxemplos* XC and XCI. Lancaster says that "the episode of the ghost may come from Plautus's *Mostellaria*, or from a play descended from it, such as Larivey's Esprits." [33] This artificial device, however, can be found in our general theme closer to home in none other than Cervantes' *Cueva de Salamanca*, where, as here, it disguises adultery or intended adultery. Not only does Dorimond have the first (and last, among works of the theme) philandering husband, but the first tutor (*docteur*)- male pupil (Léandre) relationship, one which after the time of Molière was to be made the main situation, with the tyrant as tutor or guardian and his female pupil as the object of his affection.

All of the characters are borrowed from the *commedia dell'arte:* Isabelle the *amoureuse*, the valet Trapolin, the *docteur*, the young gallant Léandre, and most especially the braggart captain. In Fa-

---

[33] *Ibid.*, p. 211.

touville's *Précaution inutile* of 1692, produced 31 years after the *Femme industrieuse,* we have already seen that the *docteur* again enjoyed the role of bystander, i. e., not actually in charge of the *amoureuse* as either husband, guardian, or brother. This immunity was to be short lived in post-Fatouville versions, for the *soldat fanfaron* seems to become forgotten as a conventional type, and the *docteur* or *docteur*-type (elderly, greedy, pedantic) comes to supplant him or be fused with him into the resultant *tuteur à clef*.

Dorimond wrote another useless-precaution play notably less clever than his first. It was *L'école des cocus, ou La précaution inutile,* whose permission to print is dated April 12, 1661,[34] seventeen days after the *privilège* of *La femme industrieuse* and about two months previous to the first performance of Molière's *L'école des maris* on June 24, 1661. The idea of an *école* was not original with Molière,[35] but there is nothing else in this play that Molière appears to have appropriated, unless it is the simple ward for his *L'école des femmes*. She, an ultimate Cervantes-type, goes back also to Zayas-Scarron as well as to Dorimond.

L'école des cocus takes place in Boulogne. The characters are again from the *commedia dell'arte*: another captain, his friend the *docteur* (who is not a tutor this time), three young ladies (Lucinde, Philis, Cloris), the gallant Léandre and his valet Trapolin. The captain gives the theme with his first lines:

> Ce siecle est si fertile en animaux cornus
> ... ...
> Qu'il faut qu'avant l'Himen ie me precautionne...

---

[34] The 1661 edition was the one used; a photostatic copy is available from the Johns Hopkins University library.

[35] Besides Dorimond's original *école* play and the two by Molière, I have compiled a list of seventeen French *école* plays and comic operas of the seventeenth and eighteenth centuries. They are mostly little-known works and unworthy of being tabulated here since only one of them, an *opéra-comique* by Rochon de la Valette entitled *L'école des tuteurs* (1754), is a true variant of the useless-precaution theme and will be examined later, as will Delavigne's post-eighteenth-century *L'école des vieillards* (1823). *L'école des mères* (1732) by Marivaux does have a simple girl like Molière's Agnès (*L'école des femmes*), one whose mother takes the role of Molière's Arnolphe; and the subject of Montfleury's *L'école des jaloux* (1664) is the curing of a jealous husband.

and then discusses this aspect of matrimony with the *docteur*. The captain wants to marry, and one by one his mistresses appear: first Lucinde who lends a vulgar turn to the play by bearing a baby then and there, next Philis whom the doctor wants to marry, and finally the simple Cloris who asks what marriage is. Naturally the captain thinks it safe to marry the naive Cloris.

Now the captain must take a trip ("...*à ma grange hors la Ville*") and leaves Cloris armed (both actions with precedent in Zayas-Scarron) so that nobody will approach her. Léandre sees her, desires her, and disarms her—again exactly as in Zayas-Scarron. He teaches her more pleasant marriage customs than the "*rudes loix*" imposed by the captain, who returns from his trip to find that he has been cuckolded. Philis and the doctor, now happily married, remind the captain what they had told him earlier: a husband's precaution is a "*chose inutile.*"

Both of Dorimond's plays are clearly Cervantes-types, yet with characters from the *commedia dell'arte*. *L'école des cocus* apparently is based on the main points from Zayas-Scarron: the surprise birth of an infant to a woman thought to be virtuous; the husband's trip; the simple wife armed and on guard; and the gallant's undeceiving her. Dorimond's two plays have the distinction of being the last ones with tyrant-husbands, to be replaced by the still-unmarried tyrant-tutor or guardian of origin in Molière. In addition to the *école* idea, the main situation of *L'école des cocus* is also that of *L'école des maris*: the aforementioned Moreto-type contrast between two opposite procedures for assuring wifely virtue. The example of the wise *docteur*'s marriage without precautions serves to emphasize the futility of the captain's treatment of Cloris; in *L'école des maris* the example of the Ariste-Léonor relationship provides contrast with the one of Sganarelle-Isabella.

II. *L'école des femmes.*

The antecedents of this play could be many.

1. Scarron. The most generally accepted source for *L'école des femmes* is Scarron's *La précaution inutile*, a version of the work by Zayas that in turn (see section on Zayas) goes back to Cervantes. It is therefore unnecessary that Molière should have

known Cervantes' *El celoso extremeño* at first hand for Cervantine inventions to appear in *L'école des femmes,* yet the critics fail to mention a possibility of ultimate Cervantine traces in Molière. I have found only one who does mention it, S. Griswold Morley, who stated in 1902 not only that "it is certain" [36] that Molière's source was Scarron, but also that the theory of *El celoso extremeño*'s having furnished traits for Molière was "utterly baseless." [37] On the contrary, *El celoso extremeño* and *L'école des femmes* have much in common.

In the first place, let us not forget that it was Cervantes who first gave to the theme its precautionary aspect, an idea which became stereotyped in the phrase *précaution inutile* beginning probably with Scarron. Both Cervantes' Carrizales and Molière's Arnolphe reveal the details of purchasing the house, outfitting it, handpicking the future wife and attempting to train her before marriage. Both seek an artless wife; both make a poor choice of servants; in fact, the weaknesses, motives, actions, and general mentality of Molière's servants Georgette and Alain correspond closely to those of the *dueña* Marialonso and of Luis in Cervantes. Cervantes' and Molière's cuckolds are truly cunning, whereas most guardians in other versions of the theme are blunderers; also these two cuckolds are rich while their wards are poor. In Molière the guardian is balked by the ward's father who returns rich from "beyond many seas." In Cervantes, Carrizales returns rich from America and negotiates with the parents of the girl. Neither parent of the ward appears in any version of the theme except in Cervantes and Molière, if we discount the different circumstances and ugly birth of the ward in Zayas. Then too there is the bribe, and at the end of both works the appearance of the notary. Certainly enough of Cervantes is in *L'école des femmes* to make a case for direct borrowing. This may be emphasized by the fact that Molière knew Spanish, as all his biographers admit, and as is attested also by the Spanish works found in his library after his death.

2. Lope de Vega: *El acero de Madrid* and *La dama boba.* As I have already tried to emphasize, Lope's only useless-precaution play was *El mayor imposible.* In a writer so fecund as he, certain

---

[36] MORLEY, *op. cit.* in fn. 27, p. 233.
[37] *Ibid.*, p. 241.

of his situations could be pointed out as previous examples of nearly any later dramatic situations. In fact, if one lends credence to Huszár,[38] one might see in Molière's three cuckold plays not only situations from *La discreta enamorada, La dama boba, El palacio confuso, Don Juan de Castro, La boba para otros y discreta para sí, El acero de Madrid, El maestro de danzar,* and *La llave de su honra*—all by Lope, but also remnants from Tirso's *Amor y celos hacen discretos,* Calderón's *El pintor de su deshonra, El astrólogo fingido,* and *El escondido y la tapada,* Alarcón's *El semejante a sí mismo,* and Moreto's *El parecido en la corte,* as well as the already-discussed *El marido hace mujer* by Hurtado de Mendoza.

Of all these plays (and others too) the two most likely candidates are *El acero de Madrid* and *La dama boba*. The former has a case of the girl's feigned illness in order to facilitate the disguised *gracioso*'s entering the house as a doctor, a part that he acts in order to be the go-between for the girl and her gallant. This play will be noted later in connection with Beaumarchais.

In *La dama boba* there is no guarding of the girl nor attempt to impose an unwanted suitor upon her; in short, there is nothing connected with Molière's useless-precaution works other than the outlandishly innocent and supinely stupid Finea, who can learn nothing from her teachers and ceases to be *boba* only when she has fallen in love. The obvious analogy is to the simplicity of Molière's Agnès.

III. *Le sicilien.*

Here is a work which many affirm to be in the Spanish taste, yet one whose sources are notably obscure. Despite its exotic setting and unusual combination of characters, this *comédie-ballet* fulfills the requisites for being a useless-precaution play. It has a jealous and precautionary guardian and a gallant's intrigue to enter the house, as well as some of the other common adjuncts to the general theme. Strangely enough, it is seldom mentioned as being

---

[38] Huszár, *op. cit.* in fn. 27, *passim.*

related to *L'école des maris* and *L'école des femmes*, yet, like them, it not only treats the same topic but also further evidences Molière's insistence that his jealous guardians be deceived *before* marriage. It may be that, from the dramatic point of view, this results in a dénouement less tragic than what developed in the quasi serious married-tyrant works which preceded Molière, but it also gives Molière's women more dignity.

As the useless-precaution theme passed from the pen of Molière to be widely imitated in his fashion, his contributions to this theme may be observed as follows:

1. The girl is neither sister nor wife to the jealous man. He is her tutor or guardian; she is his ward or choice for a wife. Practically no husband-wife useless-precaution works appear after Molière; and, to my knowledge, no useless-precaution guardian-and-ward works preceded him in French and Spanish literature.

2. Molière tends to bring into focus more the social implications of excessive male authority over women, regardless of how this authority is administered.

3. Molière originates the guardian's announced intention to marry the ward tomorrow, a device widely imitated in post-Molière works.

4. Through Molière there is a probable propagation of Cervantes-type elements of the theme either borrowed directly or having come to Molière via Zayas-Scarron.

IN THE WAKE OF MOLIÈRE

Molière popularized the theme, and nearly all useless-precaution plays subsequent to him evince his influence. Except for Fatouville's Lope-descended comedy of 1692 and another much later play by Delavigne in 1823, both the brother-sister and husband-wife relationships were to be replaced permanently by the *tuteur-pupille* one, even when the remaining elements of the intrigue are derived from sources other than Molière. In this way the topic came to be considered a French one. This stereotyping of form contributed to a general deterioration of the oft-repeated theme until in 1775 Beaumarchais suddenly raised it to an apogee, only for it to die with the beginning of the nineteenth century.

I have personally examined all the plays to be recorded here, except an elusive few which will be so indicated. All the major ones will be noted, and not a few rare minor ones; but one can be sure that other minor ones were presented but never printed, are not extant, remain hidden undiscovered in rare tomes, or are not known to me. This is particularly true of the many versions of the theme finding their way into *opéra-comique* or other musical form during the middle of the eighteenth-century heyday of the useless-precaution theme set to music.

Chronologically the first guardian-and-ward work to appear after Molière's three plays was Denis Clerselier de Nanteuil's *L'amour sentinelle, ou Le cadenats (sic) forcé*, published in 1669.[39] This play is in verse. The scene is in Paris. Florant is the *tuteur*; Isabelle, his ward; Fernant, his neighbor; Clidamant is the gallant;

---

[39] Available on photostat from the library of Johns Hopkins University.

Croctin, his valet; Lisette is the *suivante* of Isabelle; and there are other characters of less importance.

This is a weak play, with too much talk and too little action, but one with a novel twist: the jealous guardian plans to chain his ward. The gallant and his valet manage to become employed as guards in the house and beat the guardian and his neighbor when the latter pair disguise themselves and try to enter the house, thus to test the guards, who of course have recognized them. Afterwards, when the guardian and neighbor repair to the neighbor's house to change their clothes, the young lovers and their servants run off to be married. After a change of heart that was too quick, the guardian concedes the victory and even gives his benediction to the lovers as the play ends.

The author is careful not to allow the guardian actually to chain his ward as planned. Note that of all the devices in all the useless-precaution works, none is ever really cruel in the sense of physical torture for the ward or wife. Thus are the bounds of comedy maintained.

The most interesting feature of Nanteuil's play is the guardian's disguise, not the type of disguise, but the device itself. Though the beating of a disguised guardian had an antecedent in the *Cent Nouvelles Nouvelles*, heretofore disguise has been the sole domain of the gallant or his valet—and even in this play they resort to disguise—but here for the first time in the seventeenth-century manifestations of the theme the guardian pretends to be someone else. In many succeeding useless-precaution plays, the guardian will now resort to an ever more ludicrous disguise, which will ultimately develop into his being expected to don the garb of a woman at some point in the play. This not only indicates the increasing tendency to slapstick comedy, but it also accomplishes the emasculation of the already unattractive guardian. Note that in the brother-guardian series (Lope, 1615; Bois-Robert, 1653; Moreto, 1661; Fatouville, 1692), the only play in which the brother disguises himself, as a coachman, and is beaten (Fatouville's *Précaution inutile*) is also the only one postdating Nanteuil (1669). No husband or guardian disguises occur in Cervantes, Zayas, Scarron, Dorimond, or Molière. The later *Barbier de Séville*, which has no disguise for Bartholo, will in this respect revert to the earlier forms.

Also preceding Fatouville with a disguised-guardian element is the useless-precaution comedy *Le Florentin*, by either Champmeslé or la Fontaine,[40] in one act and in verse, given first on July 20, 1683.[41] It takes place in Florence in the house of Harpagême, who is the jealous Florentine to be deceived by his ward Hortense. Timante is the gallant; Agathe is Harpagême's mother; the maid of the house is Marinette; several minor characters, including a locksmith and his *garçons*, complete the cast.

The creation of the role of the guardian's mother appears to be exclusive to this play. It is rather an awkward role too. One is conditioned to picture the traditional guardian as being elderly, but here his mother's presence and advice, even though unheeded, distort the plot from its anticipated proportions. The mother counsels Harpagême to be less severe with his ward, whom he plans to marry "*ce soir*." Her words have been said so often: that no woman can be guarded "*quand elle ne veut pas se garder elle-même*."

Her son, of course, cannot be dissuaded from keeping Hortense locked up. When he has intercepted a letter from the gallant, who intended that it be intercepted, Harpagême thinks he has discovered the gallant's plans for a tryst with the ward. Then Harpagême disguises himself as a doctor, a cousin whom the ward has never seen, and who supposedly has come to exhort her to marry Harpagême. When the disguised Harpagême questions Hortense, she tells him how much she hates her guardian, whereupon Harpagême rips off his disguise. Hortense pretends to be shocked, but in reality Marinette had forewarned her of the ruse. Now the locksmith brings in an iron cage that Harpagême had ordered built to trap Timante (when he comes to see Hortense, as explained in the intercepted letter) and offers to show Harpagême how it works. Harpagême himself, however, insists on trying it. He is locked in (Timante had bribed the locksmith), all turn their

---

[40] Some writers believe that the plays attributed to Jean de la Fontaine were in reality written by, or in collaboration with, the actor Charles Chevillet, better known as Champmeslé, under whose name most of these plays are registered. Lancaster, who supports the Champmeslé authorship, summarizes the situation well in his *op. cit.* in fn. 24, pp. 487-490.

[41] A copy of *Le Florentin* is owned by the University of Michigan library.

backs on him, and the lovers gaily go off to be married. It is the mother of Harpagême who finds him in the cage and speaks to the effect of "I told you so." The play ends as the police call Harpagême to account for his excesses against Hortense and his administration of her property.

This play is sometimes mentioned as a source for Regnard's *Folies amoureuses* (1704), which we shall examine in its proper sequence. I find no specific likenesses between the two, none, that is, except the emphasis on locks, keys, and bars to be found also in other useless-precaution plays.

Probably the last seventeenth-century guardian-and-ward play was Dancourt's (Florent Carton, Sieur d'Ancourt) *Le tuteur*, given first July 13, 1695. [42] This comedy takes place in the country house of M. Bernard, who is the *tuteur* of Angelique and who in Molière-style announces to her his intention to make her his wife *demain*. For two weeks both the gallant, named Dorante, and his valet, L'Olive, have been disguised as *peintre* (cf. Molière's *Le sicilien*) and *jardinier* in the service of M. Bernard. Angelique hates Bernard and conceives the plan of telling him that the painter is in love with her, has asked her for a rendezvous that night, and that out of curiosity she has said yes. She suggests that Bernard and his trusty tenant farmer, Lucas, dress as Angelique and her maid, Lisette, and go to keep the appointment. Bernard takes the bait, unaware that he and his confidant are going to receive a beating when they keep the tryst. The humor lies in the fact that after true identification has been established, Bernard thanks Dorante for the beating, for the latter claims to have been testing the virtue of his employer's ward. At this juncture Angelique's uncle appears. When he finds Bernard in female attire he believes the accusation by Angelique's maid that both Bernard and Lucas "...*ont tous deux la rage d'être femmes.*" The uncle takes Angelique away and, at Angelique's request, he also retains the painter and gardener as well as Lisette. Bernard and Lucas are left behind to console each other.

The novel situation in this play is that the ward invents the plan for deception of her guardian. Aside from their disguises, the

---

[42] Available in Vol. 38 of a 1773 edition of *Recueil de pièces de théâtre*, owned by the University of Wisconsin library.

gallant and his valet take little initiative. The circumstances of the beating of the guardian and his confidant are different from those of the beating in Nanteuil's *L'amour sentinelle* and Molière's *L'école des femmes*; but his appearance in female attire is, as mentioned, a frequent device in eighteenth-century workings of the theme and will be seen soon again in Gueullette's *Remède à la mode*; in fact, Dancourt's whole episode here pertaining to the guardian's female disguise and beating was appropriated by Rochon de la Valette in *L'école des tuteurs* (1754), as will be seen later.

It is with Dancourt's second useless-precaution play that we pass to the eighteenth century. The work is *Colin-maillard*, in prose with scattered airs in verse, first presented on October 28, 1701.[43] As the title suggests, the game of blind-man's-buff is the high point of the play, the occasion for the gallant to whisk the ward from the house. A previous work with the same title had been written earlier by Chappuzeau but has little connection with the present work.

Robinot is the guardian. He has brought his ward, Angelique, from a convent in order to marry her (cf. Zayas-Scarron). His aunt, Mme. Brillard, advises Robinot not to force Angelique to marry him. As he is obstinate, she helps the young lovers to further their affairs, which result finally in an elopement. Eraste is the young captain in love with the ward; his valet is Lépine. Much of the acting time involves various complications between the lovers and some peasants, Mathurin (Robinot's gardener) and Claudine (Mathurin's fiancée), who threaten the lovers' planned elopement. After these complexities have been resolved, Eraste obtains a peasant's garb to join the peasants who are providing entertainment at the wedding festivities of Mathurin and Claudine. A game of *colin-maillard* takes place. Naturally the lovers escape while Robinot is the blind man.

There are several new items here: the gallant's use of a peasant disguise in order to accomplish his design; the peasants and their love affairs vying with the principal love plot; the new dignity of the aunt's role, similar to that of the mother's role in Champmeslé's *Florentin*; and the too-simple device of blind-man's-buff. There is

---

[43] A 1706 edition in Vol. VI of *Les oeuvres de Mr. Dancourt* is owned by the University of Michigan library.

nothing distinctive about either the elderly guardian or the young lovers, none of whom seems to have as much conviction of purpose as the peasants Mathurin and Claudine.

The next work is an important and successful version of the useless-precaution theme, *Les folies amoureuses*,[44] by Jean François Regnard, first given January 15, 1704. Regnard was under strong influence of the *commedia dell'arte* and is one of the most important playwrights whose comedies are gathered in the Gherardi collection from the Théâtre Italien. This three-act play is preceded by a prologue and followed by a *divertissement* with allegorical characters like those which were also common in the *commedia dell'arte*. In the body of this work, the interplay of previously-used and other extraneous devices is manipulated cleverly. Because of this and also because of the popularity which the play achieved, the plot merits analysis in detail.

Albert is the jealous *tuteur* of Agathe, whose servant is Lisette. Eraste is the gallant; his servant is Crispin. From the beginning, Agathe and Lisette are at loggerheads with Albert, constantly telling him how old and ugly and hateful he is. Two such strong feminine roles, particularly that of Lisette, may indicate that Molière's message had taken root. Indeed Albert dismisses Lisette from his service because of her sauciness but soon reinstates her, to deprive her of the pleasure which she says the dismissal gives her. When they have made their peace, Albert asks Lisette to do him a favor. He explains that Agathe is 15, that he has reared her from infancy, and that he hopes to marry her because he wants some heirs. Albert solicits Lisette's help in his project to enclose his domicile with iron bars, this to be explained to Agathe as a defense against bandits. Lisette refuses to cooperate and again tells Albert that he is mad.

When Crispin appears in front of the house and Albert inquires who he is, Crispin's reply:

> J'aurois peine à le dire.
> J'ai fait tant de métiers, d'après le naturel,
> Que je puis m'appeler un homme universel.

---

[44] I used this edition: *Oeuvres de J. F. Regnard* (Paris, 1820), Vol. III, owned by the University of Michigan library.

> J'ai couru l'univers; le monde est ma patrie:
> Faute de revenu, je vis de l'industrie,
> Comme bien d'autres font; selon l'occasion,
> Quelquefois honnête homme, et quelquefois fripon.
> J'ai servi volontaire un an dans la marine;
> Et me sentant le cœur enclin à la rapine,
> Après avoir été dix-huit mois flibustier,
> Un mien parent me fit apprenti maltôtier.
> J'ai porté le mousquet en Flandre, en Allemagne;
> Et j'étois miquelet dans les guerres d'Espagne.

not only brings to mind the braggadocio of professions, places, and accomplishments of Figaro in Act I, Scene 2, of Beaumarchais' *Barbier de Séville* (1775):

> ...fatigué d'écrire, ennuyé de moi, dégoûté des autres, abîmé de dettes et léger d'argent; à la fin convaincu que l'utile revenu du rasoir est préférable aux vains honneurs de la plume, j'ai quitté Madrid; et, mon bagage en sautoir, parcourant philosophiquement les deux Castilles, la Manche, l'Estremadure, la Sierra Morena, l'Andalousie; accueilli dans une ville, emprisonné dans l'autre, et partout supérieur aux événements; loué par ceux-ci, blâmé par ceux-là; aidant au bon temps, supportant le mauvais, me moquant des sots, bravant les méchants, riant de ma misère et faisant la barbe à tout le monde, vous me voyez enfin établi dans Séville, et prêt à servir de nouveau Votre Excellence en tout ce qu'il lui plaira m'ordonner.

rendered by the Figaro of Giovanni Paisiello's opera *Il barbiere di Siviglia* (1782) as:

> Ed io allor, per non saper che fare,
> Mi misi per le Spagne a viaggiare.
> Scorsi già molti paesi,
> In Madrid io debuttai,
> Feci un'opera e cascai;
> E col mio bagaglio addosso
> Me ne corsi a più non posso
> In Castiglia e nella Mancia,
> Nell'Asturie, in Catalogna;
> Poi passai l'Andalusia,
> E girai l'Estremadura:
> Come ancor Sierra Morena,
> Ed infin nella Galizia.

In un luogo bene accolto
E in un altro in lacci avvolto,
Ma però di buon umore,
D'ogni evento superior.
Col sol rasojo, senza contanti
Facendo barbe tirai avanti;
Or qui in Siviglia fo permanenza,
Pronto a servire Vostra Eccellenza,
Se pur io merito un tanto onor.

and converted by Rossini into the famous "Largo al factotum" for his own Figaro (1816), but it is a passage whose aspects moreover must have some connection with the servant's "catalog" speech in certain Don Juan plays.[45] Though speeches in this vein can be found also in other types of works, the element of claim to versatility and universality had its origin in the role of the braggart captain as well as in one facet of the role of Arlecchino in the *commedia dell'arte*. Apparently the *commedia dell'arte* had its influence even on the Don Juan legend; its influence on the character types in the useless-precaution plays is by now obvious.

To return to Regnard's play, Crispin later tells Eraste of the encounter with Albert, for it was Eraste who had sent Crispin "*pour sonder le terrain.*" After Crispin has been offered the usual monetary reward for his cooperation, he and Eraste lay their plans.

It seems that Agathe has not been out of the house for six months. When she complains of this, and says in addition that she wishes to marry, Albert proposes himself to be her husband. His proposal she considers impudent and she tells him: "*Je vous hais à la mort.*" Afterwards, Eraste finds a pretext to make the acquaint-

---

[45] By "catalog" is meant the enumeration of Don Juan's conquests and in what countries he attained them, all of this showing him to be the "*homme universel*," as Crispin says here. The first Don Juan "catalog" occurred not in Tirso de Molina's original *Burlador de Sevilla* (1630), but in Giacinto Cicognini's *Il convitato di pietra* (1650?), Act I, Scene 13. It is to be found successively in Molière's *Don Juan* (1665), Act I, Scene 1; Giuseppe Gazzaniga's little-known Italian opera *Don Giovanni Tenorio* (1787); Mozart's opera *Don Giovanni* (1787); Dumas père's *Don Juan Marana* (1836), Act III, Scene 4; and even in José Zorrilla's *Don Juan Tenorio* (1844). See Frank Sedwick, "More Notes on the Sources of Zorrilla's *Don Juan Tenorio*: the 'Catalog' and Stone-Mason Episodes," *Philological Quarterly*, XXXVIII, No. 4 (October, 1959), 504-509.

ance of Albert and learns that he intends to marry Agathe soon. Agathe, aided by Lisette, is now aroused to quick preventive action: feigned madness. This is a device with no past history in useless-precaution plays, unless it is a variation on the pretended illness of Belisa in Lope de Vega's *El acero de Madrid*,[46] a play to be noted in connection with Beaumarchais. With bathos, Lisette describes to Albert her mistress' grotesque actions upon seeing the locksmith (the locksmith is an element from Champmeslé or Fatouville) who had come to put up the bars. Lisette blames Albert for the supposed unbalancing of her mistress. He is crestfallen.

All of the remaining episodes exploit fully the humor to be derived from Agathe's pretended madness and its panicking effect upon Albert. First she imagines she is a singer and gives supposedly a sheet of music, but really a letter, to Eraste. She whispers to Crispin musical terms which he understands to be instructions for Eraste to come for her that night. Earlier in the play Crispin had bragged to Albert about his knowledge of science, so now Albert begs him to treat Agathe. (It might be noted that Beltrán, the valet in Lope's *El acero de Madrid*, also is a fake doctor in a similar situation; quack doctors, however, were a sure source of humor in many plays.) Next Agathe pretends to be an old lady. To pacify her, the now-indulgent Albert gives her money, which she slips to Eraste to "*avancer votre affaire.*" Then she is an army officer and in this capacity tells Crispin to get her horses, while she commands Eraste to accompany her. Eraste convinces Albert that one must humor her, and thus the lovers profit by their opportunity for escape as Crispin prescribes some strong spirits and sends Albert for them. After Albert finally discovers that he has been duped, he curses his credulity and prepares to follow the couple. This is the end of the play; but in the *divertissement* which follows, Albert finds everybody at a great party in the château of a friend of Eraste. Outwitted, he swears he will never be jealous nor even amorous again, and all are reconciled. Finis.

---

[46] Another source for the pretended madness has been mentioned as *La finta pazza*, an Italian opera, or a scenario with the same title by Flaminio Scala. See HENRY C. LANCASTER, *Sunset: A History of Parisian Drama in the Last Years of Louis XIV, 1701-1715* (Baltimore: London: Paris, 1945), p. 216.

A somewhat different variation on the useless-precaution theme appeared in 1735, different, that is, in its deviation from the usual eighteenth-century type of guardian-and-ward situation. It returns to the basic seventeenth-century type with emphasis on the would-be husband's search for an innocent wife, as in Cervantes, Zayas, Scarron, Dorimond, and Molière. In all cases the husband or guardian is duped, but in the early versions this is usually because of the wife's or ward's simplicity. As the theme became so frequently imitated in the eighteenth century, the ward tended more to become an intelligent accomplice, even instigator of the plans for deception. This notable exception, and one whose plot is different in other ways too, is *La précaution ridicule*, an *opéra-comique* by Galet first given in 1735.

Old Chrysante wishes to remarry. His first wife was a flirt, so now he seeks a simple, commonplace girl. Fourbin, the valet of his nephew, Valere, dresses as a woman and appears before the old man. This "woman" suits Chrysante perfectly. Thinking to sign a marriage contract, he signs away a *donation* to the nephew. Later when he discovers the deception, he resigns himself, reconfirms the *donation*, and gives permission for Valere to marry Angelique.

Again is seen what must have been a sure device for drawing laughter from the eighteenth-century audience: a male attired as a female, this time, however, not the old man but the valet. Per its title, this work is indeed *ridicule*, maybe etymologically *ridicule* to the audience of that time, but pejoratively so, judged as a libretto. It has a *précaution* title, an old fool looking for a simple wife, a *valet intrigant*, and a gallant who marries a young beauty; but it lacks the main element of the useless-precaution theme—the intrigue to enter the house. Some of the elements of Galet's plot recall Donizetti's Italian opera *Don Pasquale*, itself a close relative of the cuckold theme.

The next work to be examined is a *parade* attributed to Thomas Simon Gueullette (1683-1766) entitled *Le remède à la mode*, first performance before or by 1756.[47] One of the silliest of the

---

[47] Available in the 1756 edition of *Théâtre des Boulevards*, tome II, owned by the University of Southern California library. I believe this was the first printing of *Remède à la mode*, but I have not been able to authenticate its date of first performance. The work is available also from Cornell University in the 1881 edition of the same set.

eighteenth-century useless-precaution works, it evidences the mid-century deteriorization of the theme into situations which increasingly tax the imagination of the viewer or reader and strain to the breaking point the dramatist's license to extract humor from cases of mistaken identity. This tendency is not exclusive to eighteenth-century treatments of the theme. The 1661 useless-precaution works of Dorimond, for example, initiate the trend; but by now the dramatic pattern of tricking a guardian had become so well known that the writers of such plays were hard pressed to invent new and ever more ridiculous situations with which to fool the guardian and maybe extract guffaws from a cuckold-blasé audience.

The characters of *Le remède à la mode* are: Cassandre, the tutor; Isabelle, his ward; Léandre, her lover; Arlequin, valet of Léandre; and Gilles, a friend of Cassandre. In the first lines of the comedy, Arlequin complains of the hard life in serving such a master as Léandre—a device analogous to the opening complaint by the servant in the previously-mentioned (see fn. 45) Don Juan works by Molière, Gazzaniga, and Mozart. Note how increasingly saucy, even impudent, the gallant's servant becomes in the eighteenth-century plays. Thus Beaumarchais' Figaro is not an entity so novel as he is sometimes thought to be by those who identify him as the first manifestation of what was to become the spirit of the French Revolution. The seventeenth-century valets, like those of Lope, Moreto, Bois-Robert, Fatouville, and Molière, showed more restraint in their speech and more deference to their social superiors than does, for example, Gueullette's Arlequin, who in Act I says to his master Léandre: "...*le Tuteur est défiant, Isabelle est une imbécile, et vous êtes un sot*...." Then in a monologue Léandre himself laments: "*Il z'est bien triste pour un homme de condition d'avoir z'à obéir à son valet*...." How like the thoughts of Beaumarchais' Count Almaviva! The seventeenth-century gallant gave his *machiniste*, the valet, free rein without ever a qualm of this kind. The mid eighteenth-century gallant tends to be less secure in his power over the ever more bold valet and his other retainers.

Cassandre tells Gilles of his intention to marry Isabelle "*ce soir*," which later he postpones to Molière's "*demain*." One of his methods of guarding her, he says, will be to have at his door a big terrible dog which will admit only him. Léandre, dressed as a merchant, and Arlequin, dressed as an animal, accost Isabelle (who recognizes Léandre) and Cassandre (who does not). Léandre claims that it is a curious little animal from the West Indies and that it would be good for "*...garder la virginité de Mamselle votre épouse.*" Cassandre buys the animal. Naturally this Arlequin guard-animal later allows Léandre to speak sweet words with Isabelle.

Cassandre, however, overhears their plans to elope; and after the ladder has been placed at his ward's window, it is Cassandre who descends the ladder, thinking to foil these plans by having dressed as a woman. When Léandre tries to kiss what he supposes to be his ladylove, the tutor bites him and clubs him.

This plan having failed, the next one has Arlequin disguised as a roving haberdasher. When he shouts his wares, Cassandre tries to shoo him away, but Isabelle wishes to see the merchandise. Arlequin makes Cassandre try on a cap on which is written a note to Isabelle that says: "*Mamselle, dites que vous avez queuque* (sic) *chose.*" So, after Cassandre has pushed her into the house, Isabelle follows the instructions and pretends to be ill.

Some subsequent events are coarse and are quoted here only to demonstrate that the eighteenth-century pre-Beaumarchais deterioration of the theme was evident not only in the outlandish turns of plot for achieving humor, but also in the frequently lewd ideas and vulgar speech of the guardian and his allies. Now that Isabelle is thought to be ill, Cassandre sends Gilles for the apothecary. Gilles goes but says that, instead, maybe what she needs is a "*pot de chambre.*" Then Cassandre, alone, lets his thoughts wander: "*O petit Cupidon, que ne me transforme-tu dans ce moment en seringue, j'aurois le plaisir d'entrer....ah que cette idée est voluptueuse, elle me met tout hors de moi.*"

The reason for the title of the play ("*remède*") becomes apparent when Léandre, dressed as an apothecary, gains entrance to the house for the first time. He and Isabelle manage to lock themselves behind a door and in the most literal sense cuckold Cassandre. A *divertissement* and *vaudeville* follow.

The girl's feigned illness provides the opportunity for the "remedy." Compare the already-mentioned feigned illness in Lope's *Acero de Madrid* and the feigned madness in Regnard's *Folies amoureuses*. The ladder for elopement is a simple device, yet one which occurs in no other versions of the theme except those of Molière (*L'école des femmes*) and Beaumarchais. The gallant's injury in connection with the ladder originates in *L'école des femmes;* the other definite Molière trace is, of course, the "marry tomorrow."

The simple ward is not really so much "*imbécile*" as Arlequin describes her. Any simple ward is Cervantes-descended through Zayas-Scarron or Molière; but here Isabelle is simple only in that she has no plans, initiates nothing herself, says little, and does not resist Cassandre openly. In this manner, she is the reticent opposite of Regnard's enterprising Agathe.

The twice-used disguise as a merchant, with the ward asking to see his merchandise, has an antecedent in Bois-Robert and Fatouville. The device of the watchdog is both ridiculous and unique to this version of the theme; the guardian dressed in female attire occurred before in Dancourt's *Le tuteur* and will be seen again in *L'école des tuteurs* by Rochon de la Valette.

These slapstick elements, the vulgar language, the hint of an impudent valet and an apprehensive gallant, all typify the gradual transformation of the theme from its at least semi-moralizing aspect in the seventeenth century to its purely comic, and sometimes low-comic, treatment in the eighteenth century. Four more slapstick versions of the mid-eighteenth century will demonstrate the point further. They will show, in addition, another new or predominantly eighteenth-century element: the rustic setting.

One of these is an *opéra-comique* by Jean Joseph Vadé entitled *Le poirier* (1752).[48] The locale is a village on the banks of the Seine. The first scene has the usual post-Molière revelation that the *tuteur* plans to marry his ward tomorrow. The principal episode of this slight piece is as follows: The ward decides she wants to eat some pears. The gallant, disguised as a simpleton and in the employ of the guardian, is ordered by the guardian to get a ladder, place it upon the pear tree, and pick some pears. It develops, however, that the guardian climbs the ladder while the disguised gallant makes love to the ward down below. When the lovers decide that this is their opportunity, they take away the ladder. This leaves

---

[48] Available in *Biblioteque des théâtres* (Paris, 1784), Vol. XXXII, a copy of which is owned by the University of Michigan library.

the guardian up in the tree as the couple go down the river in a fisherman's boat. When much later the guardian finally is helped down from the tree by none other than the fisherman, all have assembled for the final scene. The rich *seigneur* of a nearby village brings financial pressure to bear upon the guardian, so that he is persuaded to renounce the ward. As usual, all turns out well for the ward and her gallant.

The eighteenth-century corruption of the guardian is seen not only in his often lascivious characterization, but also in his excessive greediness. Frequently he wants to marry the ward only in order to get her money. At the end of even the *Barbier de Séville*, Bartholo signs the wedding contract for Rosine and Almaviva only after it is pointed out to him that he will have the money anyhow.

A good example of the increasing importance of money to the guardian is the rather insignificant piece entitled *La pipée*, a kind of interlude with music, attributed to Clément and dated 1756.[49] This is another rustic work with the locale specified to be the countryside near Paris. Here the tutor is also the girl's uncle. She curses the fact that her father has left her to suffer the authority of this *"tiran sévère."* She wishes to marry her gallant, but the guardian will not consent because he himself wants her money. When all are out trapping birds, the guardian is caught in a bird trap and is given his freedom only after he renounces his claims upon the ward.

Another *opéra-comique* with rustic setting is *Les précautions inutiles* by Achard, given first July 23, 1760.[50] This work has sometimes been mentioned as a source for Beaumarchais. Other than the general similarity among all variants of a same theme, it is difficult to see any specific relationship between this one-act piece and the *Barbier de Séville*, except in the Scarron-derived title. Thus again it is apparent how the subtitle of Beaumarchais' play, or Achard's plural form of the phrase, does not reliably indicate derivation of plot, but rather tempts the critic to erroneous conclusions.

A country village is the setting for Achard's one-act piece. The guardian is a peasant who has reared his ward for all to believe she

---

[49] Available in *ibid*.
[50] Available in *ibid*.

is his daughter. A letter is discovered which, addressed to the guardian and signed by the Comtesse de Maranville, says that the day has finally arrived (she is arriving *demain*) on which she can take away the ward and declare that it is her daughter who had been entrusted to the peasant. Because of his greed for her money, the peasant-guardian had refused permission for his ward to marry her gallant; but all turns out well for the couple, who previously were scheming to elope, when it is discovered that they are cousins destined for each other by the Countess. So the guardian is foiled. This piece has hardly sufficient precautions or other elements of the theme to justify its title of *Les précautions inutiles*.

The fourth work of the 1750-1760 period with rustic setting, and one of a number of *école* works (see fn. 35), is an *opéra-comique* by Rochon de la Valette entitled *L'école des tuteurs*, given first on February 4, 1754, in Paris at the Théâtre de l'Opéra-Comique and published in the same year.[51] It is a close imitation of Dancourt's *Le tuteur*.

Orgon the *tuteur* plans to marry Lisette, his ward, "*ce soir*." Lisette, however, wishes to marry her gallant, Colin, and she has a plan, just like the one of Angelique in Dancourt's *Le tuteur*: she tells Orgon that Colin is to meet her in the garden at night, whereupon the tutor dresses himself to resemble Lisette and keeps the tryst with Colin, whom of course Lisette has advised of the ruse. Colin therefore pretends to be angry with the feigned Lisette. He claims to have proposed the rendezvous only to test her virtue, and now he sees that she is not worthy of him. Pretending to be very angry, Colin takes a stick and beats the poor tutor. (As we have seen, the guardian's appearance in feminine garb occurs also in Gueullette's *Le remède à la mode* and Dancourt's *Le tuteur*; the cudgeling—also in *Le tuteur* as well as in Nanteuil and Gueullette—dates from Molière's *L'école des femmes*.)

Orgon now believes he will have no trouble marrying Lisette, but a valet type named Belhumeur appears, disguised "*en robe de Palais, suivi de plusieurs satelittes*," and pretends to have come in order to remove from this village and take to jail a "*vieux radotteur, un jaloux intraitable*," who naturally is the tutor. At this junc-

---

[51] Available, as a separate edition, from the University of Minnesota library.

ture, the duped tutor genuflects at the mercy of Belhumeur, who requires him to give his purse as well as his blessing to the lovers. In addition, in true valet fashion, Belhumeur demands also money for himself. The piece ends with a little *vaudeville*. The work as a whole is singularly weak, both as a dramatic production and as an imitation of Dancourt's work.

Another little-known guardian-and-ward work, first presented in the year 1760, is the *opéra-comique* by le Monnier (librettist) and Monsigny (composer) entitled *Maître en droit*.[52] It is a rather novel version of the theme in that the guardian is a *maître en droit* in Rome. His ward is Lise. She loves Lindor.

The initial situation reminds one somewhat of the *Barbier de Séville*: the gallant Lindor is a Frenchman who has come to Rome to study law. There he sees and falls in love with the ward of this *docteur* who is his law professor. In a scene similar to the situation between Arnolphe and Horace in Molière's *L'école des femmes*, Lindor discusses with the *maître* ways to attain the favors of a young girl whom he loves. The *docteur*, like the true pedant of the *commedia dell'arte*, answers by quoting from the *Texte Romain*. He too becomes inflamed, however, and after Lindor leaves, the *docteur* wishes to be led to the apartment of Lise. The principal scene occurs when none other than Lise's governess, won over to Lindor by presents, dresses the *docteur* in female garb that she had in reality brought to facilitate Lindor's rendezvous, and leads her master blindfolded into the law school to the delight of the students. Meanwhile Lise and Lindor are joined by Law.

Next is a French work close to Beaumarchais' both in time and in its elements of plot, a version of the theme commented on by Beaumarchais himself in a preface to the first edition of his *Barbier de Séville*.[53] The work in question is *On ne s'avise jamais de tout*, by Michel Jean Sedaine, first given on September 24, 1761, in Par-

---

[52] The Library of Congress has a rare copy of this work.

[53] Beaumarchais says: "Un autre amateur, saisissant l'instant qu'il y avait beaucoup de monde au foyer, m'a reproché, du ton le plus sérieux, que ma pièce ressemblait à *On ne s'avise jamais de tout*. 'Ressembler, monsieur! Je soutiens que ma pièce est *On ne s'avise jamais de tout*, lui-même—Et comment cela? C'est qu'on ne s'était pas encore avisé de ma pièce.'"

is.[54] Sedaine's *opéra-comique* is not greatly unlike any of the other useless-precaution versions, yet it has an intangible something of spirit and mode of dénouement which seems to suggest the atmosphere of the *Barbier de Séville* and to remind us that the original form of Beaumarchais' play was that of *ópera-comique*. But *On ne s'avise jamais de tout* has no valet; and if the work was a principal source for Beaumarchais, a possibility which he did not deny, the model for Figaro had to be found elsewhere.

Like Beaumarchais' Bartholo, Sedaine's *tuteur amoureux* is a physician, a pedantic type which, descended from the *commedia dell'arte*, was always fair game for caricature on the stage. Doctor disguises are not an uncommon ruse for entering the house (e.g., Lope de Vega's *Acero de Madrid*), but here in Sedaine is the first of all the guardians previous to Beaumarchais' who is really a doctor.

This doctor is named Tue; his ward is Lise; her gallant is Dorval; her *duègne* is Margarita; there are other minor roles. The setting is a street in Paris. Much like Count Almaviva in the initial Sevillian street scene in Beaumarchais, Dorval is there in the street lamenting the fact that "*ils ne sortent point*," that he never sees Lise. Tue and the *duègne* come upon the scene, Tue checking the keys and inquiring whether all the doors are locked. The conversation turns to Tue's plans to give up his medical practice after he has married his ward, who is rich. He gives to Margarita detailed instructions of how to guard Lise whenever they go out of the house, which is only on Sundays and holidays. He shows to the *duègne* a book bought in Florence on "*comment il faut garder une fille*." Boorishly he makes her read the book aloud. (All of this has its origin in Molière's *L'école des femmes* and was used in other useless-precaution works.) At one point she reads "*les douze maximes sur les entremetteurs, commes maîtres de musique...*," etc. This could have suggested to Beaumarchais the role of Don Basile, the corrupt music master.

During the course of Sedaine's piece, Dorval has a series of three disguises: first as a domestic in the guardian's house; then "*habillé en captif, une chaîne au bras, une longue barbe blanche,*

---

[54] Available in *Recueil de pièces de théâtre*, owned by the University of Wisconsin library.

un manteau & une guitarre"; and finally "*en vieille.*" The situations are more interesting than the disguises. Each disguise allows Dorval to approach the unwitting *duègne* or talk and sigh with Lise until the guardian can be rid of him. Recall that Bartholo provides some of the best humor in the *Barbier de Séville* when he has difficulty getting rid of Almaviva, who is disguised first as a soldier attempting to lodge himself in Bartholo's house and later as a music master. (In the opera, Rossini makes capital of both these scenes as well as the "Buona sera" one where Almaviva *et al.* attempt to rid themselves of Basilio.) Sedaine has a comic trio for the scene when Dorval is disguised as a captive and the guardian is trying to dispatch this annoying supplicant. In this trio, Dorval reiterates "*charité*"; Margarita, "*liberté*"; and Tue, "*Laissez-nous....nous n'avons rien, en vérité.*"

All the hubbub at the end of *On ne s'avise jamais de tout* was to occur in Beaumarchais' play, namely, the arrival of the constabulary, the gallant's identification as a man with rank and position, and his demand to marry the ward. It is largely this identity of ending, with the presence of the police and the gallant's unmasking himself, that seems most to link Beaumarchais to Sedaine. The gallant usually comes to the fore one way or another at the end of most versions of the theme; but, except for a different type of situation at the end of Champmeslé's *Florentin* and another at the end of Cervantes' *El viejo celoso*, the final arrival of the constabulary is unique to Beaumarchais and Sedaine.

A Spanish guardian-and-ward work intervened between Sedaine (1761) and Beaumarchais (1775), one which Beaumarchais might have known at first hand. It is the *zarzuela* by Ramón de la Cruz entitled *El tutor enamorado*, first presented in Madrid at the home of the Marquis d'Ossun, the French ambassador to Spain.

The occasion of this performance was the marriage of María Luisa, daughter of Charles III, to Pedro Leopoldo, the Archduke of Austria, who later became Leopold II, Emperor of Germany. This performance took place shortly before Beaumarchais arrived in Madrid in May, 1764. He stayed in Spain until March, 1765. From the standpoint of his interests and the company which he kept in Madrid, it is not improbable that Beaumarchais saw a later performance of this *zarzuela*, or at least heard of it, or maybe read it, especially since Beaumarchais knew M. d'Ossun, the French ambassador, and dined almost daily with him while he was in Madrid.[55]

I have not succeeded in examining a copy of *El tutor enamorado*, but the plot is summarized in Cotarelo y Mori's study of Ramón de la Cruz.[56] This *zarzuela* apparently has both the rustic and incredulous elements that gained prominence in the French eighteenth-century useless-precaution works. Here the guardian isolates his ward in a "*casa de campo*," but by means of both magic and a *tercera* the gallant manages to enter the house and speak with the ward. The guardian suddenly returns from a trip (one of the oldest and most-used Cervantes-type elements) and surprises the lovers; but before he can incarcerate his ward in a convent, she is carried off, again with the aid of magical arts. Finally the ambition and avarice of the tutor are unmasked and he must consent to the marriage of the ward and her gallant. The reader will agree that this is hardly a work to compare to Beaumarchais'.

The guardian-and-ward play closest in time to Beaumarchais' *Barbier de Séville* is Cailhava's *Le tuteur dupé*, in five acts and in prose, first given on September 30, 1765, in Paris.[57] This play was revived in 1773, the same year in which the *Barbier de Séville* was approved by the censor and received at the Comédie-Française. (*Le barbier* had been written a year earlier in 1772 but was not actually performed until 1775.) In Cailhava's preface to the edition of 1778, he confesses to have based his play on the framework of Plautus' *Miles gloriosus*, which, through the Italian *commedia dell'arte*, had supplied so many boastful captains to the French stage. Cailhava's guardian, however, is not a soldier, nor is there anything military in the play.

Le tuteur dupé is another useless-precaution comedy with rustic setting "*près d'un village aux environs de Paris.*" Richard is the guardian of Emilie. Her *femme-de-chambre* is Marton; Richard's valet is Merlin. Contrary to custom, Damis the gallant has no valet; but, like Almaviva in the *Barbier de Séville*, he makes use of

---

[55] LOUIS DE LOMÉNIE, *Beaumarchais and His Times* (New York, 1857), p. 94; also RENÉ DALSÈME, *Beaumarchais* (New York: London, 1929), p. 56.
[56] EMILIO COTARELO Y MORI, *Don Ramón de la Cruz y sus obras* (Madrid, 1899), p. 57.
[57] A 1781 edition is available from the University of Michigan library.

the valet employed in the house. In addition to a domestic, a notary, and his clerk, there are Mme. Argante, who is Emilie's aunt, and Grégoire, who is Richard's gardener. Recall the guardian's mother in Champmeslé's *Florentin* (1683) and his aunt in Dancourt's *Colin-maillard* (1701). Middle aged or elderly women are infrequent characters in useless-precaution plays. Here for the first time the ward is given an aunt. Although her role is a slight one, this aunt is the first relative of any kind that the ward has had since the works of Cervantes and Molière. There have been several gardeners before, for example, in Dancourt's two guardian-and-ward plays.

The plot is similar to Plautus' play mainly in the mode of deceiving the undesired suitor. Cailhava has the adjoining houses and the secret opening between them to facilitate the girl's changes of attire and disguises as her own twin sister. This situation was only one incident in Plautus, but in Cailhava it is the core of the play. Like Figaro, the conniving valet Merlin is given much prominence, but so have other valets originated most of the intrigue in other versions. The guardian is made to believe that his ward's sister (Emilie's disguise) wants to marry him. He insists on marrying Emilie but consents that the sister marry his rival, Damis. By means of one of the usual tricks with the marriage contract, the guardian unwittingly signs for his ward to marry her gallant. Thus he is duped; furthermore, he finds himself married to Emilie's aunt.

The most significant feature of this play is that Cailhava apparently wished it to be one of his principal efforts, else he would not have troubled himself to write an eleven-page preface nor to develop the old hackneyed guardian-and-ward plot in the elaborate fashion that he did. There is nothing slight in this play; Cailhava attempts to motivate his situations as well as make them and his characters plausible. It is not an outstanding play; but, judged among its kind (useless-precaution comedies), it is clearly a step forward from the beatings and some of the impossible situations of the theme at mid-century. It remained for Beaumarchais to give us the sanest version of them all, the one in which the characters indeed think as well as act.

Le barbier de Séville or *La précaution inutile* came from the pen of that gay French factotum, Beaumarchais, as an *opéra-comique* in 1772. Never presented in this form, because the actors had refused to appear in it, finally it was performed on February 23, 1775, Beaumarchais having converted the original verse dialogue to prose and having expanded the work to five acts. Result: complete failure. Still resolute, Beaumarchais revised the piece, eliminated some of the crude dialogue, reduced it to the original four acts, and shortly thereafter had it presented again, this time successfully. So popular was *Le barbier* in this last form that its translations are hardly fewer than its numerous imitations and adaptations. Of all these, the best known is Gioacchino Rossini's opera *Il barbiere di Siviglia*, libretto by Cesare Sterbini, first performance Rome, 1816. This opera itself is an imitation of a previous one by Giovanni Paisiello, with the same title and first given in what is now Leningrad, 1782. It was Rossini, however, who gave spontaneity of score to what had been Beaumarchais' gift for vivacity of dialogue and action.

Seemingly the *Barber of Seville* is not really the story of a barber, nor does Seville appear to be important at first sight. These two elements, however, can be linked. Although a rather recent institution in the long history of human society, the barber shop has been since its inception a place for gossip and banter. The barber himself has long ago been typed as a garrulous individual, informed on most matters of the moment, and often with a goodly stock of anecdotes. Entertaining barbers have reappeared constantly in European literature since the Middle Ages. Some of the oldest barber tales can be found in the *Thousand and One Nights*, where the voluble and rascally Es-Sámit (whose name means "the silent one"!) is akin to Figaro.

Barbering may already have been introduced into the Iberian peninsula before the Moors arrived in 711. The Greeks and Romans had barbers, but among the Arabs barbering was an important part of daily life, hence the many colorful barbers in Arabic tales. When the Arabs brought their civilization to the Spanish peninsula, Seville was one of the cities in which the Moorish customs arrived earliest and in which the Moors remained longest. Even today the city of Seville retains some of its oriental atmosphere; and it may have been adroitly chosen that Figaro should be not only a barber, but a barber of Seville. In Beaumarchais' preface to the first edition of the *Barbier de Séville*, he admitted to have wanted at first "...*d'écrire et de faire jouer la pièce en langage espagnol...pour rendre la vraisemblance encore plus parfaite...*"; but on second thought he felt compelled to write it in French after all because "*...tandis que la vraisemblance exigeait qu'il s'étayât sur les mœurs espagnols...*" the foreign language would cause it to lose its gaiety for the French public.

It is perhaps erroneously though none the less more generally believed that Beaumarchais laid his plot in Spain, rather than France, not necessarily because he had lived in Spain and indeed knew and liked Spain well, nor because the Spanish code of honor did in reality require that woman be guarded, but rather to use the locale as a smoke screen for Figaro's jibes at French nobles and institutions. Yet the presence of Figaro scarcely affects the fundamental plot: the gallant and his ladylove might have found their own means, as they did in Sedaine's *On ne s'avise jamais de tout*. It is tone which Figaro gives to the play. By the time of Beaumarchais, the theme required the new spice of something like a Figaro in order to postpone its demise, now that the culture which spawned the theme was wearing out in an epoch which presaged civil rights for women, including the unchallenged prerogative of a young woman to choose her husband. Thus, in a sense, Beaumarchais revived the theme. It could not last, however, except preserved in the garb of opera, where all themes are timeless and all things are possible. If Molière's addition to the theme was the change of husband to guardian and wife to ward, better to demonstrate the social aspects of excessive male authority over women, Beaumarchais' contribution is his shift of emphasis to the role of valet and its social aspects.

There have been many theories on the origins of Figaro. His role of *entremetteur* surely is nothing new and could have been modeled after that of certain Spanish *graciosos* and French valets in the previous workings of the theme, particularly Gueullette's saucy valet whose independence does not pass unnoticed by his master. It is Figaro's personality, however, that interests us and distinguishes Beaumarchais' work from the rest of similar works with similar roles for the go-between. Can it not be that Figaro is none other than Beaumarchais himself? Based on the facts of Beaumarchais' life, this is a logical conclusion at which to arrive, because few men have ever lived a more intense life or exhibited so many divers talents.

The son of a Protestant watchmaker, Pierre-Agustin Caron was born in Paris in 1732. Later in life he added to his name the appellation Beaumarchais, by which posterity has come to know him. His formal education had terminated at the age of thirteen, and after an adolescence spent as watchmaker's apprentice Beaumarchais was overcome by social ambition. Nothing could stop him. His letters, a fecund index to his personality, reveal the same innate gaiety, wit, and intelligence that sparkle in the characterization of Figaro, if his role is properly acted, or that carry over into Rossini's opera when properly sung.

Like Figaro, Beaumarchais was a man of many professions. He invented a watch. He was a talented harpist at the court of Louis XV. He was a diplomat, then a business man who grew rich through speculation. Although posterity knows him chiefly as a dramatist, he was also a song writer. He was involved in many intrigues and once was brought to a court of law on an accusation of slander, so the well-known calumny passage of the play (made into a principal aria, the "La calunnia" crescendo, for Don Basilio in the opera) may well be the result of personal experience. Beaumarchais killed a man in a duel, dabbled in politics, and had three wives besides many mistresses. Finally he was exiled. Beaumarchais became very rich during his life but died a poor man in 1799, ruined by the same French Revolution whose spirit Figaro embodies.

More than any other version of the useless-precaution theme, Beaumarchais' play evidences a composite of sources. In an earlier publication [58] I have already indicated the influence of Spanish music, manners, and literature upon Beaumarchais as well as the comparison to be drawn between Cervantes' *El celoso extremeño* and Beaumarchais' *Barbier de Séville*, the conclusion being that the latter owes more to Spain than is generally acknowledged. Even so, the *Barbier de Séville* has enough complexity in its specific situations of plot to defy claims of *exclusive* descent from any posited single source.

Mainly for this reason it is impossible to accept the attractive

---

[58] For a more detailed comparison of these two works see Frank Sedwick, "Cervantes' *El celoso extremeño* and Beaumarchais' *Le barbier de Séville*," *The French Review*, XXVIII, No. 4 (February, 1955), 300-308.

theory offered by Florence N. Jones in 1908, in her already cited (fn. 6) *Beaumarchais and Plautus: The Sources of the Barbier de Séville*, that Beaumarchais consciously and deliberately took Plautus' aforementioned (see p. 15) *Miles gloriosus* as a plot model to be imitated in detail, only with the characters and types of situations naturally brought up to date. On her page 13 Miss Jones mentions also "the resemblance" between the *Barbier de Séville* and *Le tuteur dupé*, which Cailhava admitted to be an imitation of Plautus' *Miles gloriosus*. First of all, even were Beaumarchais to be conceded a gift in the art of camouflage, the skeleton plot of the *Barbier de Séville* seems to be quite different from that of either the *Miles gloriosus* or Cailhava's *Tuteur dupé*, even though some of the trappings in Beaumarchais are similar to Cailhava's; e. g., the gallant who, himself without a valet, buys for cash the services of the valet of the house; also the marriage-contract scene, etc.[59] Secondly, if one is to maintain that Plautus' play sired Beaumarchais', the latter being in a double sense—time and stature—practically the end product of the whole genre, why not count certain others (or all) of the numerous pre-Beaumarchais guardian-and-ward comedies to be among the Plautus progeny?—which is to deny any exclusive rights of inheritance to Beaumarchais. That is to say: if Beaumarchais' play came from Plautus, the others could have the same origin; and if they did, any theory of Beaumarchais' direct indebtedness to Plautus is untenable. Even though it has already been stated early in this history that Plautus' comedy probably did supply one of the characters to the *commedia dell'arte*, the boastful captain, who found his way into some of the useless-precaution plays, there is insufficient reason to believe that Plautus' plot as a whole gave origin to the theme itself or to any of its numerous variations.

---

[59] Miss Jones erroneously bases part of her argument for Beaumarchais' imitating Cailhava on the fact that (her p. 13), she says, Beaumarchais wrote "...his comic opera *Le barbier de Séville* in 1773, the same year in which Cailhava's *Tuteur dupé* was put again upon the stage...," and that "...seeing the success of his contemporary's play, [Beaumarchais] resolved to remodel his play after Plautus...." The reasoning of in-sight, in-mind, is always a plausible argument; but, even though it was never presented, Beaumarchais had written his original version of *Le barbier* not in 1773, but in 1772, one year before the revival of *Le tuteur dupé*.

Among Beaumarchais' French sources closer at hand, the principal one appears to be Sedaine's *On ne s'avise jamais de tout* and not—other than the general similarities of the theme among all useless-precaution works—the works of Scarron, Dorimond, Regnard, Achard, Fatouville, or even an opera by Panard (*Le conte de Belflor*), as it has been so often claimed. After all, Beaumarchais himself did not disallow the affinity of his play to that of Sedaine (see fn. 53); and, as we have already seen, several of the situations in *On ne s'avise jamais de tout* correspond closely to those in the *Barbier de Séville*. What was most notably lacking in *On ne s'avise jamais de tout* was a valet; but the originality of Figaro, even if not his function, has been already acknowledged.

There is nothing specific of either Scarron, Fatouville, or Achard in the *Barbier de Séville* except the subtitle. Dorimond had a *docteur* in his two cuckold plays, but not one who was matched with a ward or wife in the usual fashion; Sedaine's ward is the first to have a doctor as her guardian. Regnard and Gueullette do have valets conceivably forerunners of Figaro; Regnard too has a ladder for the elopement, as does Beaumarchais, but so does Molière (*L'école des femmes*).

Molière's two *école* plays are usually mentioned as a source for most post-Molière useless-precaution plays. It has already been stated that Molière popularized the theme and that the later variations of the theme do show some influence of Molière. Yet, except for the decision to "marry tomorrow," Beaumarchais appears to have passed over the two *école* plays in favor of certain situations in *Le sicilien*, which was a musical piece like the original form of the *Barbier de Séville*. There are four uncommon elements that Beaumarchais might well have taken from *Le sicilien:*

(1) the gallant and his musicians serenading the imprisoned ward;

(2) the appearance of the guardian in his nightcap (Molière) or at the balcony in the early morning (Beaumarchais);

(3) the gallant's stratagem of the fabricated letter of introduction in order to gain admittance to the house; and

(4) the servant's distraction of the guardian while the gallant makes love to the ward in the same room.[60] Numbers 1, 2, and 4

---

[60] In connection with this element, S. Griswold Morley made an interest-

occur in no other versions of the theme except *Le sicilien* and *Le barbier*; number 3 was used in the Lope-types, but there the bearer of the letter was the valet instead of the gallant. One additional element possibly from Molière is Count Almaviva's disguise as a substitute music master, which has an antecedent in *Le malade imaginaire*, a play not included in our theme.

Strictly speaking, Lope de Vega's *El acero de Madrid* is not a useless-precaution play either, although it was mentioned earlier in connection with Molière's *L'école des femmes*, Regnard's *Folies amoureuses*, and Gueullette's *Remède à la mode*. *El acero de Madrid* does have a *gracioso* who dresses as a doctor in order to enter the house, but it is mostly a certain something in the spirit of the dawn scenes in Lope's play that reminds one of the opening scene in *Le barbier de Séville*. Note also the middle of Lope's Act II where outside the house Riselo twice shouts "¡*Ah de casa*!" In *Le barbier* when in Act II the Count comes to the house disguised as a drunken soldier, he shouts "*Réveillons-là!*" rendered in Rossini's opera (Act I, Scene 9) as "*Ehi di casa*!"[61]

---

ing parenthetical observation in his "Notes on Spanish Sources of Molière," *PMLA*, XIX (1904), 289. He mentions the *entremés* entitled *El borracho* of the early seventeenth-century *entremesista* Luis Quiñones de Benavente as follows: "This brilliant *entremés* seems like the third act of *le Barbier de Séville* turned inside out. There is a barber, but he is the Bartholo, a suspicious old man with a pretty daughter. Figaro, fertile in plots, is a soldier, who gets shaved while his friend the gallant entertains the lady. While waiting for the shaving implements to be brought, the soldier, quite like Rosine, sings verses alluding to the events actually taking place. The song absorbs the old man's attention, but he arouses himself in time to see the lover take his daughter's hand. It is explained to the father that the girl is merely having her fortune told. The shaving process gives the young people more opportunity, and finally the soldier feigns to become drunk and falls on the floor. While the barber seeks some one to carry the fellow out, the gallant escapes with the lady, and the soldier with the money sack. Crude as this is compared with such a refined product as *le Barbier de Séville*, in reading it for the first time one is startled into believing one has seen it all before; yet upon opening one's Beaumarchais one finds there not a phrase, hardly a word, which might indicate a possible connection."

[61] It is in the rest of this scene in the opera that the only principal operatic deviation from the play occurs. In the opera, when the confusion in this scene requires the arrival of the police, the disguised Count whispers his rank to the police officer, who then discreetly retires. In Beaumarchais, no police have come, and the Count does not persist in lodging in the house. He has left without further disturbance, after having got the note to Rosine, as Rossini's hero had also done. Probably the opera must have the scene

It is scarcely possible to speak of Beaumarchais' play without reference to Rossini's opera, which in my opinion has been largely responsible for projecting the French original beyond its social, stylistic, and thematic confines of the late eighteenth century, not to mention the analogous perpetuation of Beaumarchais' sequel through Mozart's *Nozze di Figaro*. Perhaps thus Beaumarchais' fame has come somewhat by chance in his having had good imitators or adaptors. Certainly Figaro himself is more widely known from Italian opera than from his originally French incarnation. Before the opera was written, however, the theme was to be reworked one more time in Spain.

This presumably last Spanish manifestation of the theme is a neatly constructed, fresh and clever *sainete* by Juan Ignacio González del Castillo entitled *La inocente Dorotea*, with date c. 1800.[62] In this work the extreme simplicity of the ward, Dorotea, may have had a model in Lope de Vega's *La dama boba* or in Molière's *L'école des femmes*.

In Molière's play, the ward says things which make Arnolphe split his sides with laughter; e. g., do children come through the ear? Later, after she has been wooed by Horace, Arnolphe asks Agnès whether Horace did any more than kiss her arms. She replies: "Why! Do people do other things?" This is the point at which Arnolphe lectures Agnès on the need for wifely obedience in their future married life and has her read a volume of maxims of mariage. (Sedaine in *On ne s'avise jamais de tout* availed himself of this element from Molière.)

With regard to Lope's play, it has been stated already that *La dama boba* is not really a useless-precaution work, but the humor of the question-and-answer scenes from its Act I bears comparison to that of certain equally funny passages in *La inocente*

---

with the police because by this time it needs a lusty chorus. In Beaumarchais, the constabulary (*alguazils*) do not arrive until Scene 8 of the fourth and last act. Aside from this difference, Rossini and his librettist followed the play closely, although sometimes they reversed the order of certain scenes; they omitted little but did reduce verbiage. After all, unlike Beaumarchais, Rossini had no political ax to grind.

[62] Available in *Obras completas de Don Juan Ignacio González del Castillo* (Madrid, 1914), Vol. I.

Dorotea. Lope's simple girl is named Finea; Laurencio, in need of money, has decided to court her. She interrogates him thus:

> FINEA. ¿Qué es amor?
> LAURENCIO. ¿Amor? Deseo.
> FINEA. ¿De qué?
> LAURENCIO. De una cosa hermosa.
> FINEA. ¿Es oro, es diamante, es cosa
> destas que muy lindas veo?
> ....
> FINEA. Pues, ¿llevaráme a su casa
> y tendráme allá también?
> LAURENCIO. Sí, señora.
> FINEA. ¿Y eso es bien?
> LAURENCIO. Y muy justo en quien se casa.
> Vuestro padre y vuestra madre
> casados fueron ansí.
> Deso nacistes.
> FINEA. ¿Yo?
> LAURENCIO. Sí.
> FINEA. Cuando se casó mi padre
> ¿no estaba yo allí tampoco?
> LAURENCIO. *(aparte)*
> ¿Hay semejante ignorancia?

In the *sainete* by González del Castillo, Dorotea is by far the most innocent of her kind. She has been secluded to the extent that she has never seen a man. She is moved to inquire about men, love, and marriage after she has discovered a picture of Narciso (the gallant) placed by her *dueña*, Felipa, where Dorotea will be certain to find it. (The portrait was a Lope element also in *El mayor imposible*.) Dorotea of course falls in love with the portrait and inquires:

> DOROTEA. Dígame usted: ¿qué animal
> es el que tiene una cara
> tan parecida a la nuestra?
> FELIPA. Ese es el hombre....
> ....
> DOROTEA. Y dígame usted, los hombres,
> ¿Para qué sirven?
> ....
> ¿Y abundan mucho?
> FELIPA. No faltan;

IN THE WAKE OF MOLIÈRE

>   Cada mujer tiene el suyo,
>   aunque también hay mil damas
>   que los tienen a docenas.
> DOROTEA.   Pues haga usted que me traigan
>   uno siquiera.

The guardian, Jacobo, who has reared the orphaned Dorotea since her infancy, wants to marry the ward in order to appropriate her large inheritance. His plan is to prevent Dorotea ever from seeing a young or handsome man so that she will think an old and homely one, namely him, to be a prize. In the words of Jacobo:

> Si una niña, por desgracia,
> al abrir los ojos ve
> un asno, la idea se arraiga;
> y, siendo moza, se muere
> por unas orejas largas.
> Si es papagayo el que mira,
> no hay remedio, no le agradan
> los amantes que no tienen
> la nariz acaballada.

His plan goes awry because of the usual opposition: the gallant's servant, Pedro, has entered the service of Jacobo in order to facilitate Narciso's entrance into the house to woo Dorotea; and the *dueña* Felipa has joined the conspiracy. Because this *sainete* postdates Beaumarchais' play, it is not surprising to find the gallant's aide in the employ of the guardian, although this was also the case in the Lope-types.

Pedro suggests to the guardian that the latter visit Dorotea dressed as an angel in order to be all the more impressive. Jacobo concurs and insists that Pedro accompany him dressed as a devil, for contrast thus to make the guardian even more acceptable. The scheme fails because in the meantime the ward has seen, in person, and loved Narciso; and of the ridiculously attired angel Dorotea says:

> ¡Ay qué cara
> tan horrorosa! ¡Qué feo!
> ... ...
> ¡Pero si usted me horroriza
> más que esotro [the devil]!

As in some other versions, the notary arrives. Narciso is to marry Dorotea; Pedro is to wed Felipa.

This *sainete* has the guardian's Molière-descended decision to marry the ward without delay, or as Jacobo says here, "*casarme hoy sin falta.*" Another item of interest is the age relationship between the guardian and his ward. In all versions except the brother-guardian plays derived from Lope, there is assumed to be significant disparity in age between the guardian and his ward. Here it is stated precisely that Jacobo is 70 and Dorotea 16. In both Cervantes' *El viejo celoso* and *El celoso extremeño*, the jealous husband is exactly 70; the wife, 15.

If *La inocente Dorotea*, written about 1800, closes the account for Spanish use of the theme, one may assume that beyond this time such a topic was incompatible with the changing social outlook and its reflected new themes and techniques of the new century. The eighteenth century in Spain, as in France, had been one in which the social practices of real life were but little removed from the manners staged in the ever less exemplary and ever more superficial versions of the useless-precaution theme. The Frenchified aspects of eighteenth-century Spain are well known, and the word *afrancesado* applied to Spanish manners of that time testifies to a kind of dandyishness. There is mingled with the plot of *La inocente Dorotea* some biting criticism of these customs of the day, the type of satire with which Ramón de la Cruz had earlier seasoned his hundreds of one-act pieces. The more sober atmosphere of liberalism and reform in nineteenth-century Spain was not one conducive to perpetuation of outworn literary themes, especially one tied to mores of a previous century with which writers were attempting to break their bonds.

For the French at least, these bonds were broken at the turn of the century with the French Revolution, in the spirit of which Western mankind still attempts to live. Even Beaumarchais' *Barbier de Séville* of 1775 was one of many types of factors contributing to the advent of this French Revolution. It is interesting that, to my knowledge, only one variation of the useless-precaution theme appeared in the French language after the French Revolution; and, as one might expect, on the basis of the line of reasoning proposed here, it is a serious play devoid of the usual seventeenth- and eighteenth-century trappings of go-between, bribe, disguise, guardian's decision to marry tomorrow, and other stereotyped elements. It lacks so conspicuously the customary elements that it may not seem at first glance to belong to our theme. Closer scrutiny identifies it as a curious descendant of Molière's *L'école des maris.*

The reference is to Casimir Delavigne's *L'école des vieillards*, a play first given December 6, 1823.[63] A mature and thoughtful work, it pictures two men with different ideas on whether an old man should marry.

The setting is Paris, and the play commences with the meeting of Danville and Bonnard, old friends who have not seen each other for a long time. Danville, age 60, discloses that he has married for the second time; in fact, his son is three years older than his new wife, who is about 20. This leads the two friends to discuss the advisability of marriage at their age. Danville is supremely happy with his remarriage, while Bonnard defends his life of a celibate.

As the plot unfolds, marital difficulties arise for Danville in the person of the Duc d'Elmar, who makes love to Danville's young wife. She considers the Duke to be impudent and presumptuous, but this cannot prevent the scheduling of a duel between the Duke and Danville. Now, however, it is for Danville to be astonished and disapproving when Bonnard informs his friend that he himself is going to marry. All turns out well when Danville's own wife demonstrates her faithfulness by dispatching the Duke.

Danville does not take any of the traditional useless precautions, nor is his wife simple; she is merely capricious and in this way arouses his jealousy. Apparently the ridiculous precautions of the seventeenth- and eighteenth-century workings of the theme were by 1823 out of mode to the extent that they are totally omitted in a work like this one, which nevertheless bears in its title the *école* of yore. Even more important, the nineteenth-century gallant, the Duke, is repulsed. This fact alone sounds the death-knell of the theme.

---

[63] Available in his *Oeuvres complètes* (Brussels, 1838), owned by the University of Chicago library.

SUMMARY

What became popularized as a French-type theme had previous examples in Spanish literature, with ultimate sources traceable through the literature of the Eastern Mediterranean back to the Orient.

The two channels for propagation of the theme from Spain were Cervantes and Lope de Vega.

With his translation of the Cervantes-descended work of María de Zayas, Scarron probably gave the theme its name of *précaution inutile*. The wide currency which these words later acquired as a set phrase, especially in the titles and subtitles of dramatic variations on the theme, makes them unreliable as an indication of source for any given post-Scarron versions of the useless-precaution theme.

The influence of the Italian *commedia dell'arte* upon this theme is more one of character names and character types than one of plot.

Molière standardized the theme with a guardian instead of a husband (Cervantes) or brother (Lope de Vega); he was also the first to give the theme any social significance.

After the time of Molière, the theme became popularized and frequently vulgarized, especially during the middle of the eighteenth century. This trend commenced toward the end of the seventeenth century when the guardian began to acquire disguises, particularly feminine ones.

When deterioration seemed nearly complete, Beaumarchais wrote his *Barbier de Séville*. With the fame of this play, enhanced and even perpetuated by Rossini's operatic version, the useless-precaution theme reaches its apogee. Molière had elevated the role of the ward; Beaumarchais embellished the role of the valet.

After Beaumarchais and the French Revolution, the theme was to die of old age, its trappings and even basic features incompatible with the new atmosphere of nineteenth-century France and Spain.

FRANK SEDWICK
ROLLINS COLLEGE, WINTER PARK, FLORIDA

BIBLIOGRAPHY

Books

ACHARD. *Les précautions inutiles.* Available in *Biblioteque des théâtres* (Paris, 1784), Vol. XXXII, a copy of which is owned by the University of Michigan library.
ALFONSO, PEDRO (PETRUS ALPHONSI). *Die Disciplina Clericalis des Petrus Alfonsi,* ed. by Alfons Hilka and Werner Söderhjelm. Heidelberg, 1911.
BEAUMARCHAIS, PIERRE AGUSTIN CARON DE. *Oeuvres complètes.* Paris, 1845.
BOCCACCIO, GIOVANNI. *Il decamerone.* 3 vols. Genoa, 1913.
BOIS-ROBERT, FRANÇOIS LE METEL DE. *La folle gageure.* Paris, 1653. Available in the U.S.A. at the libraries of these universities: Princeton, Cornell, Johns Hopkins, Chicago, Kansas, and California (Berkeley).
BONILLA Y SAN MARTÍN, ADOLFO. *Entremeses de Miguel de Cervantes Saavedra.* Madrid, 1916.
CAILHAVA. *Le tuteur dupé.* Available in *Théâtre de M. Cailhava* (Paris, 1781), Vol. 1, a copy of which is owned by the University of Michigan library.
CALDERÓN DE LA BARCA, PEDRO. *Comedias.* 4 vols. Leipzig, 1827-1830.
CERVANTES SAAVEDRA, MIGUEL DE. *El celoso extremeño. Novelas ejemplares,* II, 87-171. Madrid, 1943.
CHAMPMESLÉ (pseu. of CHARLES CHEVILLET), or authorship by LA FONTAINE, JEAN DE. *Le Florentin.* Paris, 1683. The University of Michigan library owns a copy of this play.
CLÉMENT. *La pipée.* Available in *Biblioteque des théâtres* (Paris, 1784), Vol. XXXII, a copy of which is owned by the University of Michigan library.
CORDIER, HENRI. *Bibliographie des oeuvres de Beaumarchais.* Paris, 1883.
COTARELO Y MORI, EMILIO. *Don Ramón de la Cruz y sus obras.* Madrid, 1899.
DALSÈME, RENÉ. *Beaumarchais.* New York: London, 1929.
DANCOURT (FLORENT CARTON, SIEUR D'ANCOURT). *Colin-maillard.* Paris, 1701. Available in a 1706 edition of *Les oeuvres de Mr. Dancourt,* Vol. VI, owned by the University of Michigan library.
———. *Le tuteur.* Paris, 1695. Available in Vol. 38 of a Paris, 1773, edition of *Recueil de pièces de théâtre,* owned by the University of Wisconsin library.
DELAVIGNE, CASIMIR. *L'école des vieillards. Oeuvres complètes.* Brussels, 1838. Available from the University of Chicago library.
DORIMOND. *L'école des cocus, ou La précaution inutile.* Paris, 1661. Johns Hopkins University library owns a photostatic copy.
———. *La femme industrieuse.* Paris, 1662. Johns Hopkins University library owns a photostatic copy.

FATOUVILLE, NOLANT DE. *La précaution inutile. Théâtre italien*, I. Paris, n. d.
LA FONTAINE, JEAN DE, or authorship by CHAMPMESLÉ (pseu. of CHARLES CHEVILLET). *Le Florentin*. Paris, 1683. The University of Michigan library owns a copy of this play.
GONZÁLEZ DEL CASTILLO, JUAN IGNACIO. *La inocente Dorotea. Obras completas*, I. Madrid, 1914.
GONZÁLEZ PALENCIA, ANGEL. "El celoso engañado," *Historias y leyendas*. Madrid, 1942.
———. "Juicio de Menéndez Pelayo sobre la *Disciplina Clericalis*," pp. xxxv-xxxviii of González Palencia's bilingual (Latin and Spanish) edition of the *Disciplina Clericalis* (Madrid: Granada, 1948), a reproduction of the Hilka-Söderhjelm text *Die Disciplina Clericalis des Petrus Alfonsi* of Heidelberg, 1911.
GUEULLETTE, THOMAS SIMON. *Le remède à la mode*. Available in *Théâtre des Boulevards* (Paris, 1756), Vol. II, a copy of which is owned by the University of Southern California library; the Cornell University library owns a copy of the 1881 edition of the same collection.
HURTADO DE MENDOZA, ANTONIO. *El marido hace mujer. Biblioteca de autores españoles*, XLV (Madrid, 1881), 421-436.
HUSZÁR, GUILLAUME. *Molière et L'Espagne*. Paris, 1907.
JONES, FLORENCE N. *Beaumarchais and Plautus: The Sources of the Barbier de Séville*. Chicago, 1908.
LANCASTER, HENRY C. *A History of French Dramatic Literature in the Seventeenth Century*. 6 vols. Baltimore, 1926-1936.
———. *Sunset: A History of Parisian Drama in the Last Years of Louis XIV, 1710-1715*. Baltimore: London: Paris, 1945.
LINTILHAC, EUGÈNE. *Histoire générale du théâtre en France*. 5 vols. Paris, 1904-1911.
LOMÉNIE, L. DE. *Beaumarchais et son temps*. 2 vols. Paris, 1856.
MARTINECHE, ERNEST. *La comédie espagnole en France de Hardy à Racine*. Paris, 1900.
———. *Molière et le théâtre espagnol*. Paris, 1906.
MOLIÈRE. *Oeuvres*. 2 vols. Paris, 1877.
LE MONNIER (LIBRETTIST) and MONSIGNY (COMPOSER). *Maître en droit*. Paris, 1760 (?). The Library of Congress owns a rare copy of this *opéra-comique*.
MORETO, AGUSTÍN. *No puede ser el guardar una mujer. Biblioteca de autores españoles*, XXXIX (Madrid, 1911), 187-208.
MORILLOT, PAUL. *Scarron et le genre burlesque*. Paris, 1888.
MORLEY, S. GRISWOLD. *The Interludes of Cervantes*. Princeton, 1948.
———. *Spanish Influence on Molière*. Doctoral dissertation. Harvard University, 1902.
NANTEUIL, DENIS CLERSELIER DE. *L'amour sentinelle, ou Le cadenats (sic) forcé*. Paris, 1669. Johns Hopkins University library owns a photostatic copy which bears an undecipherable date, either 1672 or 1675.
PLAUTUS, TITUS MACCIUS. *Comoediae*. 2 vols. Oxford, 1952.
PUIBUSQUE, A. *Histoire comparée des littératures espagnoles et françaises*. Paris, 1843.
REGNARD, JEAN FRANÇOIS. *Les folies amoureuses*. Available in *Oeuvres de J. F. Regnard* (Paris, 1820), Vol. III, a copy of which is owned by the University of Michigan library.

ROCHON DE LA VALETTE. *L'école des tuteurs*. Paris, 1754. Available from the University of Minnesota library.

RODRÍGUEZ MARÍN, F. *El Loaysa de El celoso extremeño*. Sevilla, 1901.

SÁNCHEZ DE VERCIAL, CLEMENTE. *Libro de los enxemplos. Biblioteca de autores españoles*, LI (Madrid, 1912), 443-542, ed. by Pascual de Gayangos; also *Libro de los exenplos por a. b. c.* (Madrid, 1961), ed. by John E. Keller.

SCARRON, PAUL. *La précaution inutile. Oeuvres de Scarron*, III, 233-280. Paris, 1786.

SEDAINE, MICHEL JEAN. *On ne s'avise jamais de tout*. Available in Vol. 13 of a Paris, 1773, edition of *Recueil de pièces de théâtre*, owned by the University of Wisconsin library.

VADÉ, JEAN JOSEPH. *Le poirier*. Available in *Biblioteque des théâtres* (Paris, 1784), Vol. XXXII. a copy of which is owned by the University of Michigan library.

VEGA CARPIO, LOPE DE. *Obras*. 15 vols. Madrid, 1890-1913.

ZAYAS Y SOTOMAYOR, MARÍA DE. *El prevenido, engañado*, in *Novelas amorosas y ejemplares*, Barcelona, 1646, a copy of which is owned by the University of Chicago library.

ARTICLES

BOHNING, WILLIAM H. "Lope's *El mayor imposible* and Boisrobert's *La folle gageure*," *Hispanic Review*, XII (1944), 248-257.

BOURLAND, C. B. "Boccaccio and the *Decameron* in Castilian and Catalan Literature," *Revue Hispanique*, XII (1905), 1-232.

CIROT, GEORGES. "Gloses sur les 'maris jaloux' de Cervantes," *Bulletin Hispanique*, XXXI (1929), 1-74.

KELLER, JOHN E. "The *Libro de los exenplos por a. b. c.*," *Hispania*, XL, No. 2 (May, 1957), 179-186.

KRAPPE, ALEXANDRE H. "Les sources du *Libro de exemplos*," *Bulletin Hispanique*, XXXIX (1937), 5-34.

MORLEY, S. GRISWOLD. "Notes on Spanish Sources of Molière," *PMLA*, XIX (1904), 270-290.

PLACE, EDWIN B. "Beaumarchais and Bibliography," *The French Review*, XXIX, No. 1 (Oct., 1955), 58.

―――. "María de Zayas, an Outstanding Woman Short-Story Writer of Seventeenth Century Spain," *University of Colorado Studies*, XIII, No. 1 (June, 1923), 1-56.

SEDWICK, FRANK. "Cervantes' *El celoso extremeño* and Beaumarchais' *Le barbier de Séville*," *The French Review*, XXVIII, No. 4 (Feb., 1955), 300-308.

―――. "More Notes on the Sources of Zorrilla's *Don Juan Tenorio*: the 'Catalog' and Stone-Mason Episodes," *Philological Quarterly*, XXXVIII, No. 4 (Oct., 1959), 504-509.

SYLVANIA, E. V. "Doña María de Zayas y Sotomayor: A Contribution to the Study of Her Works," *Romanic Review*, XIV (1923), 199-232.

VEGA CARPIO, LOPE DE. *El mayor imposible*, ed. by John Brooks, *University of Arizona Bulletin*, V, No. 7 (Oct. 1, 1934), 1-209.

www.ingramcontent.com/pod-product-compliance
Lightning Source LLC
Chambersburg PA
CBHW020422230426
43663CB00007BA/1271